# A Tale of No Name

**Author**
Wing Shing Ma

**Translator**
Yun Zhao

**Editors**
Shawn Sanders
Kevin P. Croall

**Production Artist**
Hung-Ya Lin

**US Cover Design**
Hung-Ya Lin

**Production Manager**
Janice Chang

**Art Director**
Yuki Chung

**Marketing**
Nicole Curry

**President**
Robin Kuo

*www.comicsworld.com*

English translation by
ComicsOne Corporation 2004

**Publisher**
ComicsOne Corp.
48531 Warm Springs Blvd., Suite 408
Fremont, CA 94539
www.ComicsOne.com

**First Edition: July 2004**
**ISBN  1-58899-376-0**

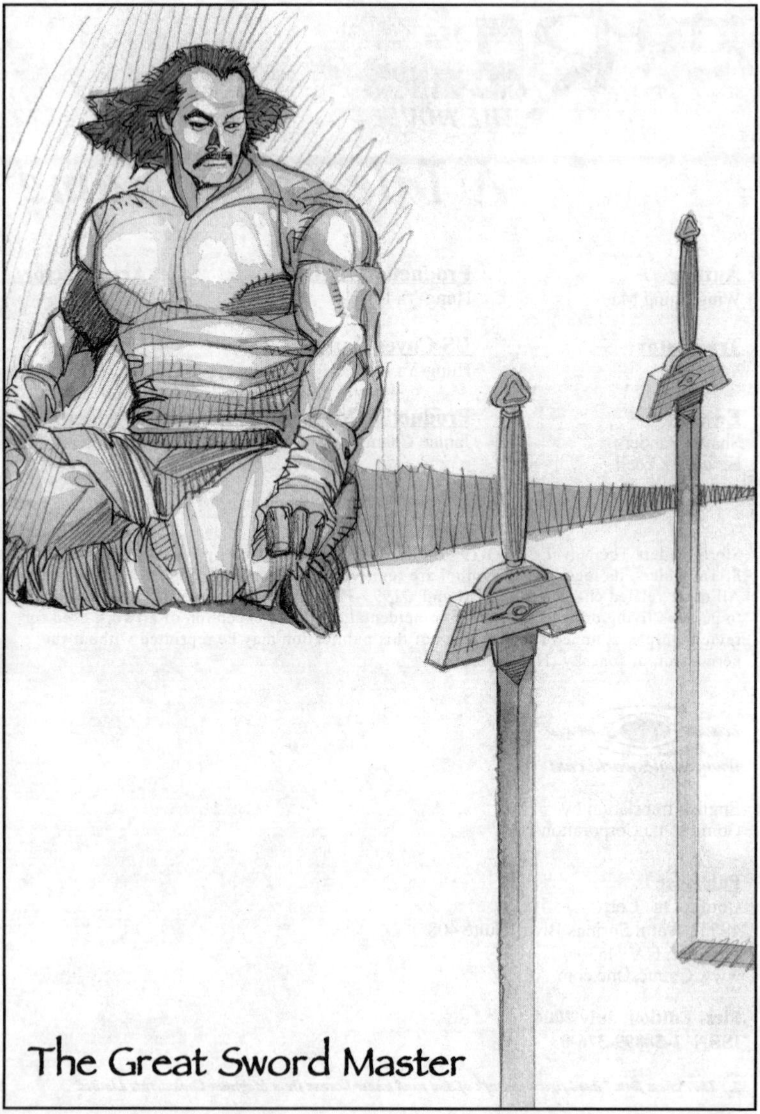

The Great Sword Master

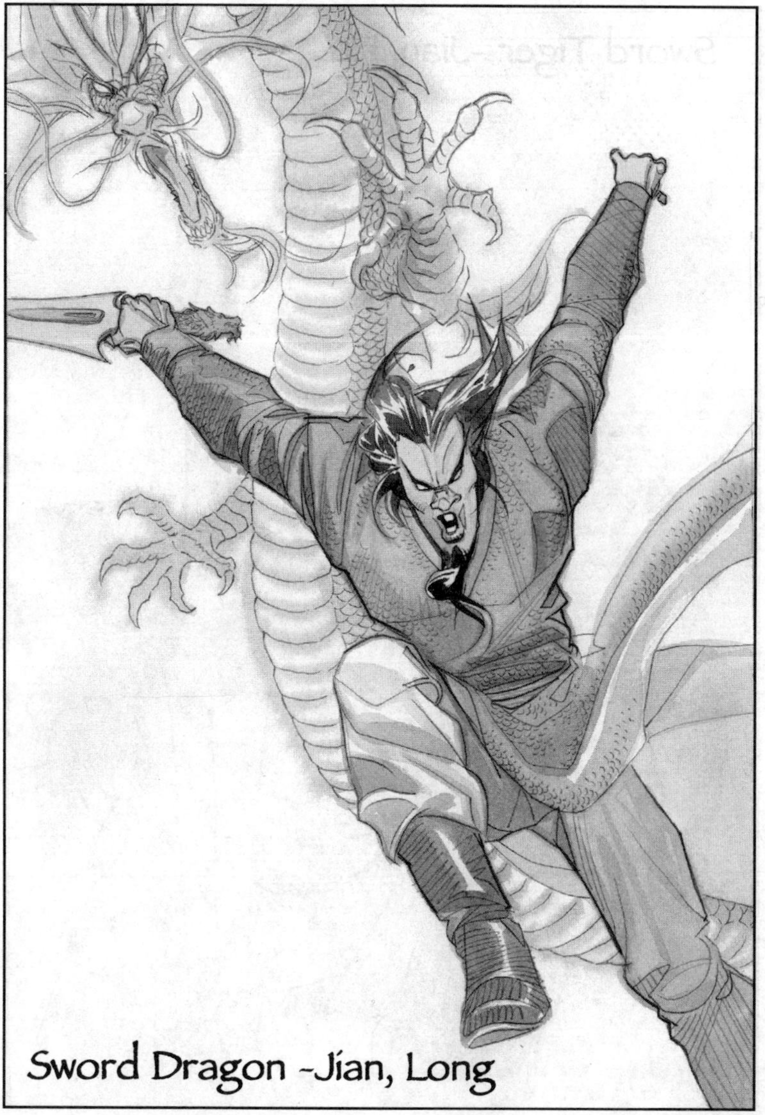

Sword Dragon -Jian, Long

Sword Tiger -Jian, Hu

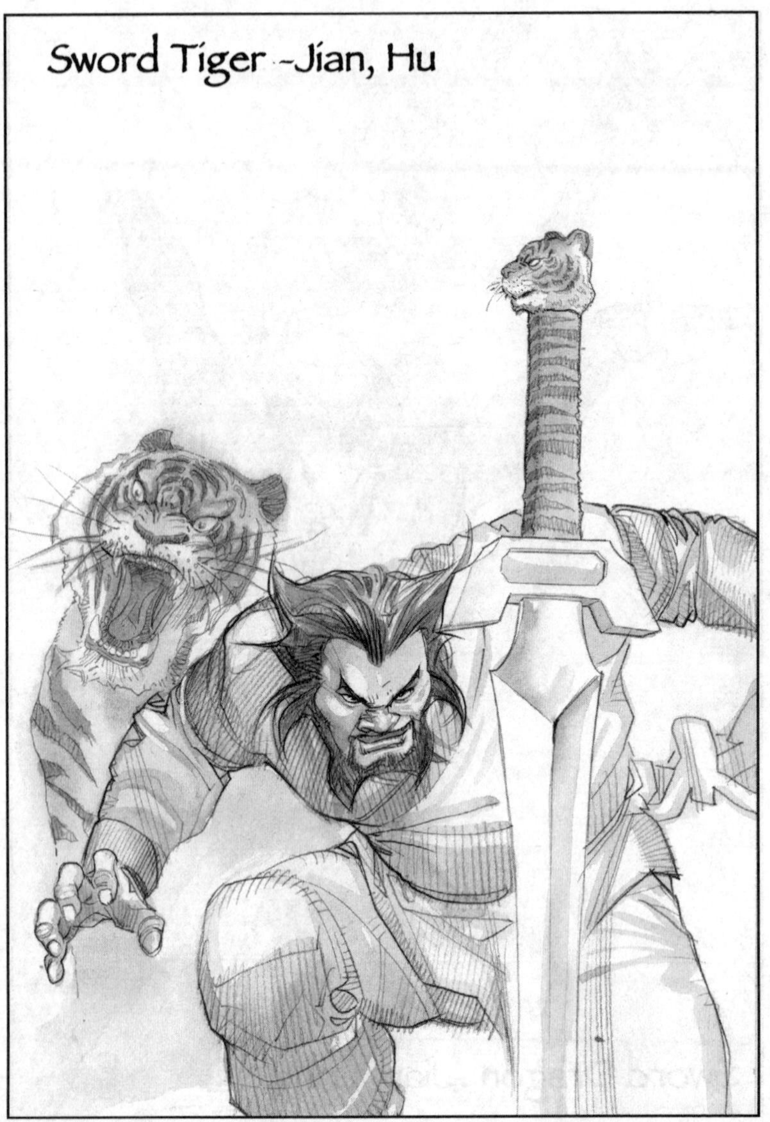

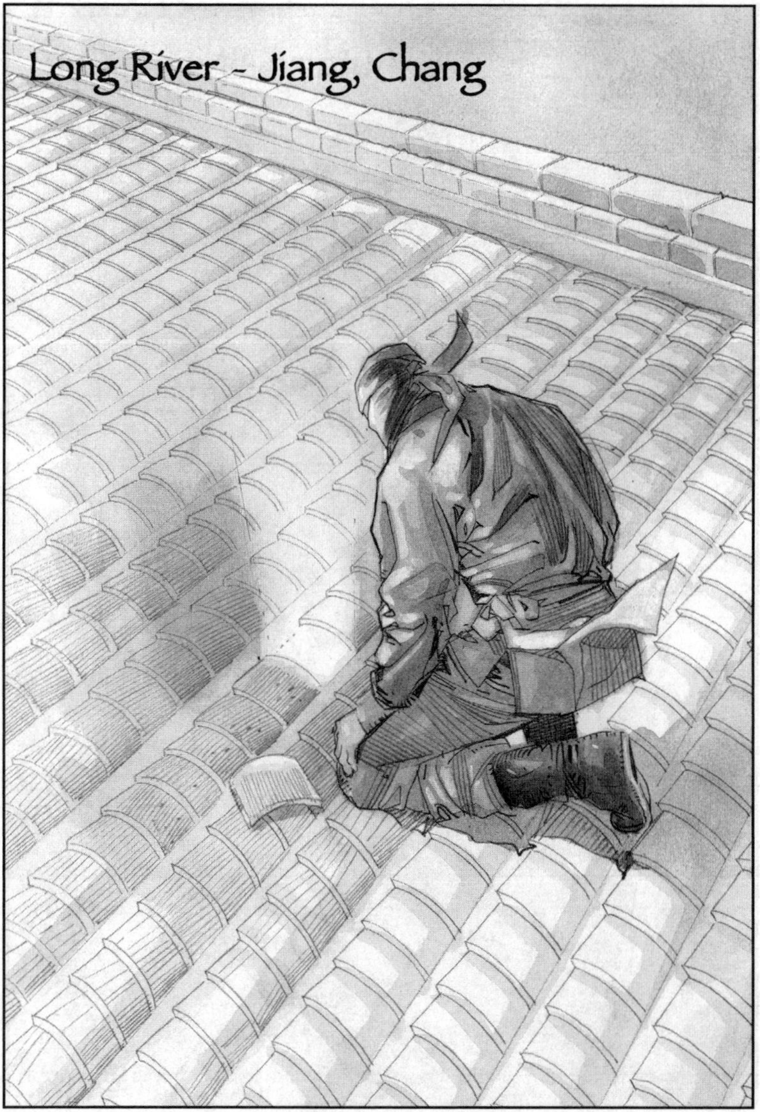
Long River - Jiang, Chang

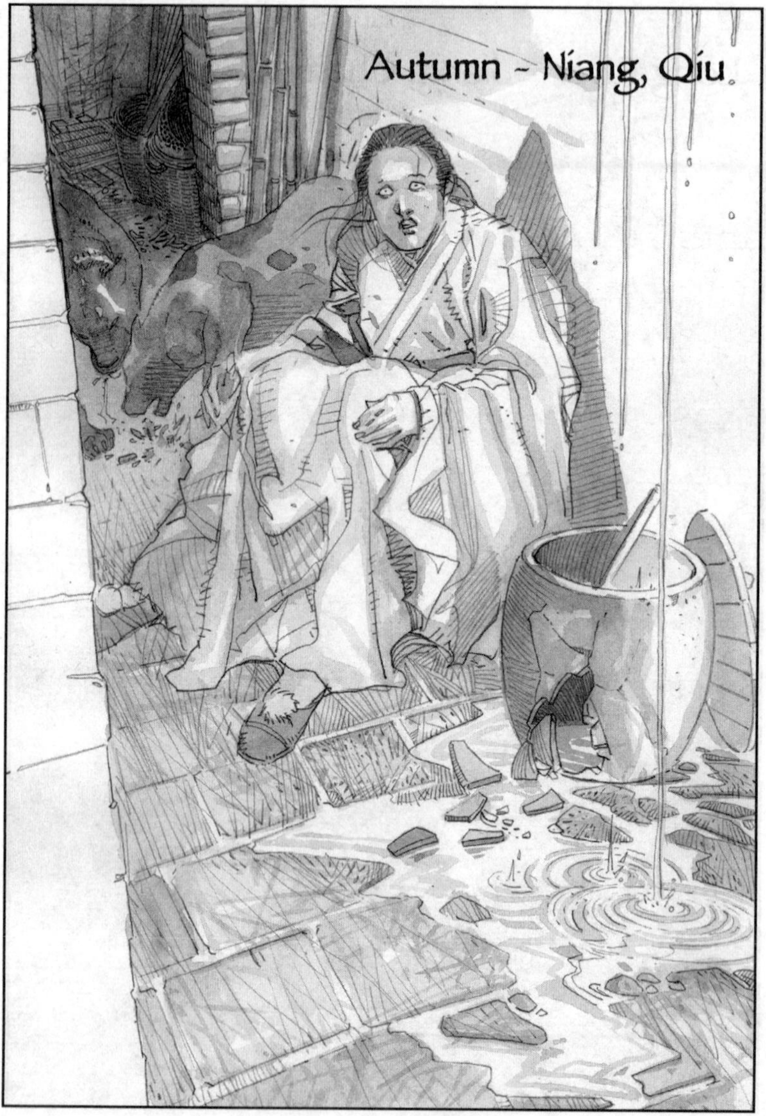
Autumn - Niang, Qiu

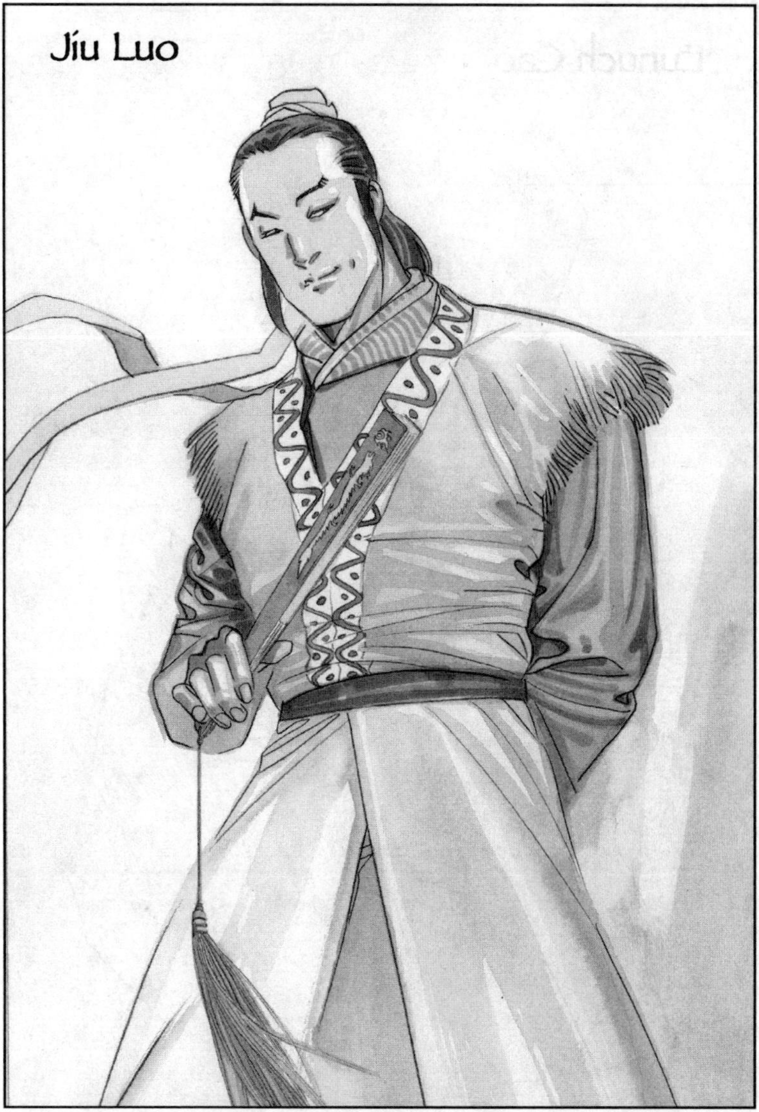
Jíu Luo

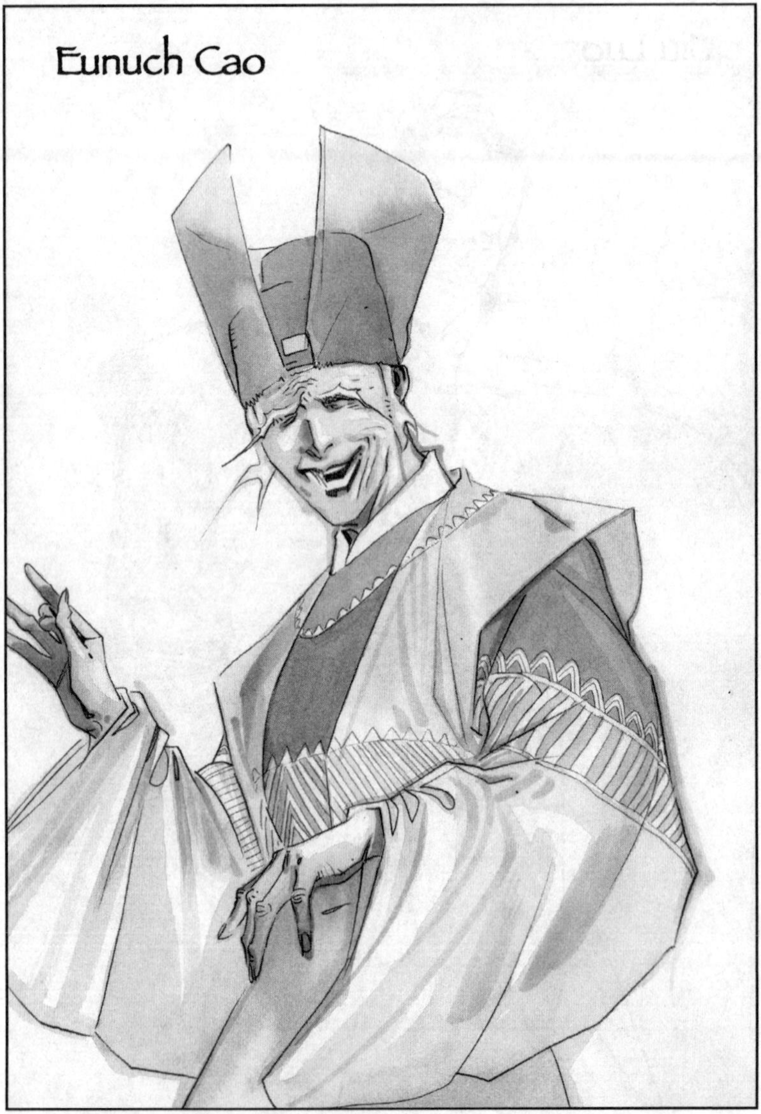
Eunuch Cao

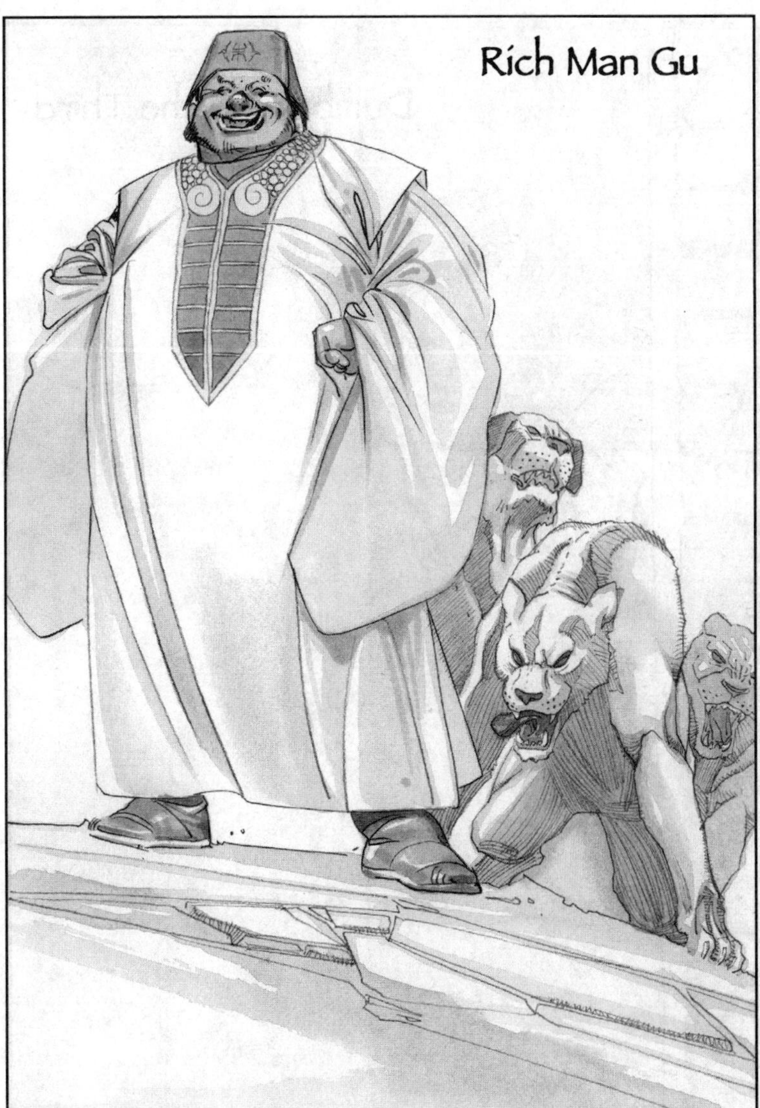

Rich Man Gu

# Dumb Head the Third

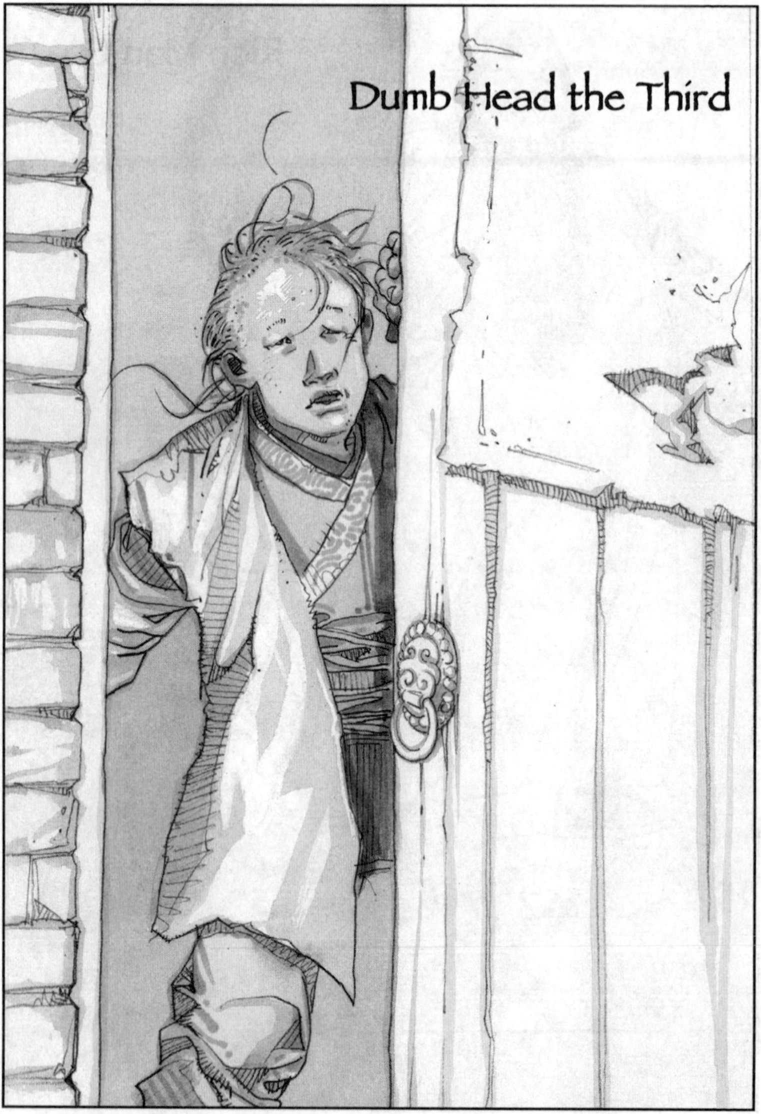

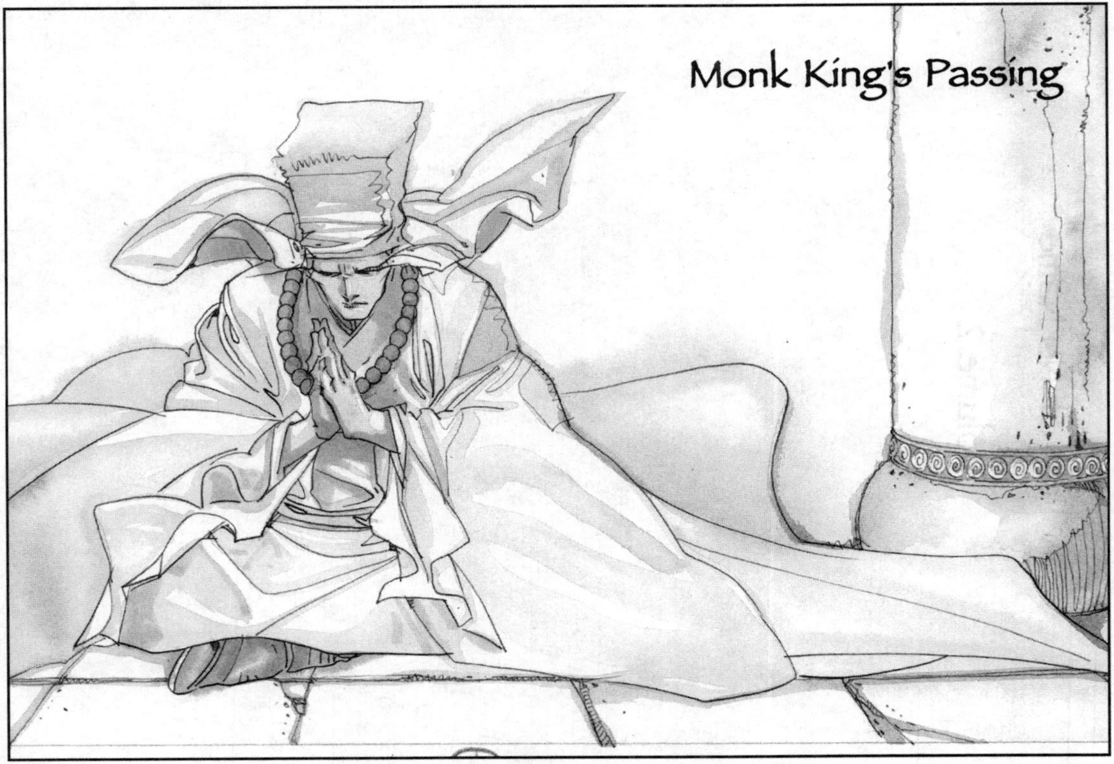
Monk King's Passing

# A Tale of No Name

## Volume 2

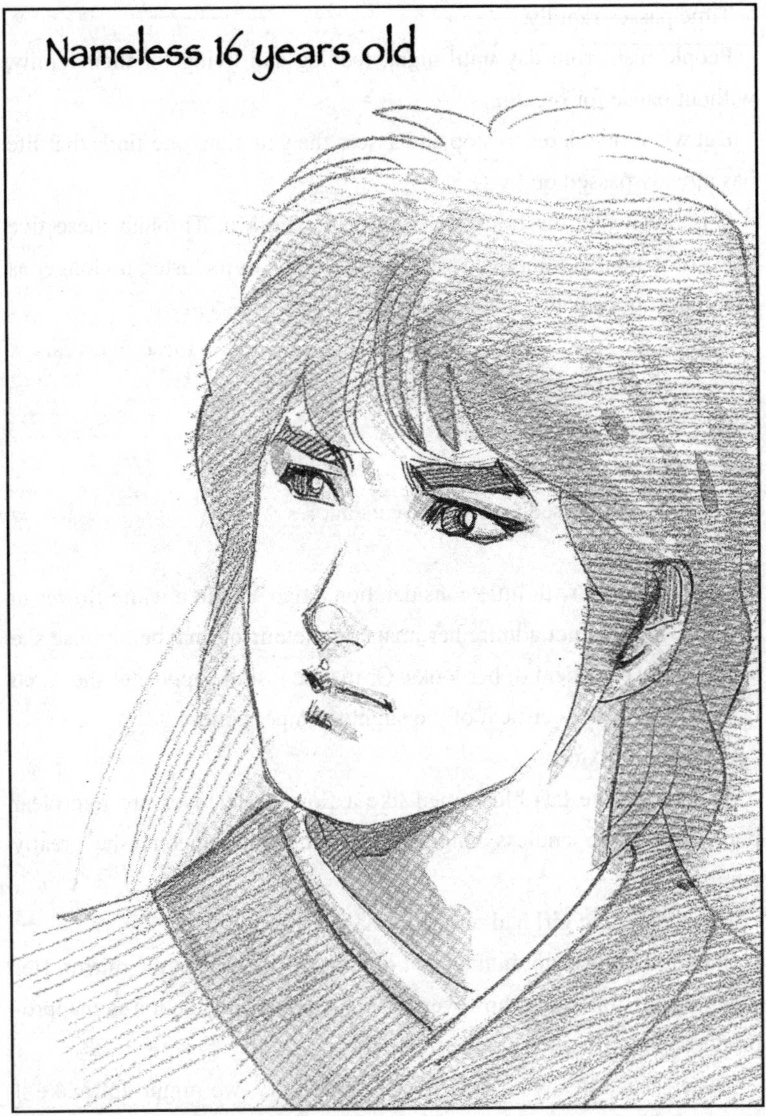
Nameless 16 years old

Time passes rapidly.

People rush from day until night, feeding and living for their family, without pause for breath.

But when one dares to stop and assess the situation, one finds that life has already passed on by...

It is much like the bricks making up Castle Mu. Through these five years of wind and rain, the Castle has lost some of its luster, no longer as grand as it once was.

And each of the castle residents has also changed in these five years...

Perhaps, the only one who didn't change...

Was *him*.

And *him*.

Madame Mu passed away five years ago...

Carelessly and with little consideration, Xiao Yu put a white flower in her hair. She did not admire her image in the mirror, maybe because she was already confident of her looks. Or maybe just the opposite; she cared too much to look -- critical of the slightest imperfection.

She is now sixteen.

At sixteen, she has blossomed like a flower. Her eyes are like clear pools, hiding an endless longing, a longing for someone she greatly admires.

The cute young girl had turned into a true beauty!

But Xiao Yu was not in the habit of admiring herself in the mirror. Her older sister Chiu Hong, however, on a day when such action is inappropriate, sat admiring her visage in the mirror.

"Sister, it is already so late, if you don't hurry, we might not make it there today."

Yet Chiu Hong did not relinquish her mirror.

"All right, all right!" she answered impatiently, "Why are you always in such a rush, Sis? Is it such a big deal? We're just going to "Wife-Yearning Cliff" to mourn auntie. Don't you think I should be properly attired and look my best?"

Today marks the fifth year anniversary of Madame Mu's death, and it is also her birthday. Xiao Yu had promised long ago to accompany Hiro and pay respects on this day. She had always admired and respected her aunt.

But as the departure time drew near, Chiu Hong delayed further, and the time was pushed back again and again. Xiao Yu began to grow anxious.

"Sister, our aunt was so kind to us when she was alive. We owe it to her to visit her grave once a year in hopes to pay back her generosity. How can you ask if it is a big deal?"

Chiu Hong was momentarily stunned. She did not expect her sister would talk back to her in defense of their aunt.

"Bah! You're too loyal!" she retorted. "No wonder Brother Hiro always wants to be with you! Forget it then, I'll go and help you kiss up to Hiro!"

"Sister…" Xiao Yu's face turned red with disappointment. She realized now that her older sister cared nothing for their aunt, or for her. She didn't know how to react. Just then a voice called out.

"Chiu Hong! Since you don't think praying for my dead mother is a big deal, then you don't need to go! Just stay here with your… mirror!"

A rush of chi pushed the two sisters' door open, and continued into the room. It impacted onto Chiu Hong's cooper mirror and left a deep hand-print, as if slapping the reflected image of Chiu Hong in the mirror.

At the same time, someone entered the room. Before the sisters could discern the intruder, Xiao Yu's hand was grabbed and she was led out.

But Xiao Yu did not show any sign of fear, because she already knew who this person was.

It was Hiro!

In the five long years, Hiro had already grown into a strong, extraordinary young man. He was tall and handsome, and the corner of his mouth seemed always turned up in an unconscious expression of pride. He had become the very vision of any young woman's ideal husband.

The only thing that had not changed in the last five years was his long unbound hair, his snow white robes, and his prideful glance!

His glance was the same as it was five years ago, a look that seemed to peer into the hearts of men.

Chiu Hong pleaded behind them, but Hiro ignored them. He continued pulling Xiao Yu along, as if he were a man with an iron heart.

The show of chi left on the mirror and his great speed as he rushed into the room to lead Xiao Yu away, revealed how his martial arts had improved in the last five years. But his candidness and enthusiasm only suggested that his real potential had yet to be realized.

The aura of the ruler of swords emanated from him, stronger than it had five years ago!

Being pulled so close to Hiro as they traveled brought a blush to Xiao Yu's face. She asked, "Brother Hiro, are we really leaving my sister behind?"

Hiro showed his proud face and answered, "If she really wanted to see my mother, she would have been prepared. I don't need such an insincere person! I only need you!"

Need her? Xiao Yu's face registered shock. Hiro thought her irresistibly cute, but did not want to lead her on. "Sister Xiao Yu," he added, "don't misunderstand me! I need you to go with me to pray for my mother, because you are very sincere!"

Is she ugly? No, she is not at all ugly! Just the opposite, she is beautiful in every sense of the word. It's just that she is unaware of her beauty. Her sister Chiu Hong who sits all day primping in front of the mirror, hoping that she can make herself a little prettier, was terribly jealous of her sister's good looks.

Xiao Yu knew that it was useless to argue with Hiro, so she tried another topic.

"Brother Hiro, will uncle be coming with us today?"

Hearing this question, Hiro's prideful glance lowered slightly.

"He… won't be coming this year. He's very busy."

Mu Long had been busy lately, and had not been to his dead wife's grave in over two years.

Love is always thus! In the first year after her passing, Mu Long thought of her constantly; the second year and third year, he still thought of her often; but by the fourth year…

He immersed himself in his work, and began to forgo visiting her grave!

Love is always thus!

Passion and ardor always pass, fading with time.

But Mu Long was retired, so what exactly had him so busy night and day?

Xiao didn't ask for details, and knew that her uncle Mu Long holed himself up in conference with his advisor Bao, constantly. It seemed as if they were discussing something important. Xiao Yu was curious, but she did not pursue it.

And Hiro seemed uninterested in discussing it further.

"Sister Xiao Yu, my father will not be coming, it will just be you and I. Are you afraid of being alone with me?" He's always teasing her.

Xiao Yu's face turned scarlet, as she shook her head.

"No, we won't be alone, there is one other person, if you don't mind, and I've asked him to come along."

Who is the "him" Xiao Yu mentioned? Hiro already knew, and his face changed.

"What? You invited him? And he agreed?"

Xiao Yu smiled kindly.

"Brother Hiro, you should know that although you have never gone with him to visit your mother all these years, he has still gone alone. His devotion for your mother is clear to see! I know that he's been trying to avoid you, but I told him auntie's spirit in heaven would be so happy to see both of her sons there today, together as a family. How do you think he reacted? He agreed without any hesitation."

Hiro gave a cold laugh.

"Really? But you did not think to ask me if such a despicable person could come along with us?"

Xiao Yu ignored his reaction and continued kindly.

"I was sure you would have agreed. Although you don't want to be near him, I know you also would want mother to smile down on us from heaven, right? It would make her happy."

Hiro looked at her, as if staring into her heart. After a long moment, he responded.

"You're right."

"I will allow him to come along for the sake of my mother."

Hearing him agree, Xiao Yu smiled. At the same time, the two reached the gates of Castle Mu and saw *him*.

He was standing solemnly, waiting outside the door.

It's been five years! But he is still the same as he was then!

Standing silently outside the door, watching everyone's life, death, love...

Hate! He has hardly changed!

Aside from growing as tall as Hiro, his aura is still the same as before, filled with sorrow, an endless sorrow.

The only change is with his head that he vowed he would never lift up. As Madame Mu wished, he now holds his head high.

But it no longer mattered if he lifted or bowed his head! The reason that he did so for long ago was because he didn't want anyone to see his "hero's face" and that preternatural sword potential...

But, the extraordinary light and aura have completely disappeared.

In their place, was the guilt and regret of believing himself to be the cause of Madame Mu's death.

His aura has been completely dissolved by his guilt and regret!


Wife-Yearning Cliff.

It is situated twenty miles out side of Castle Mu. Legend calls it a place of lost love.

During the Tang Dynasty, there was a scholar who wished to become an official in the Capital, but lacked the funds for the examination. He was filled with knowledge, but could do very little with it.

Knowing her husband's dilemma, his wife secretly worked in a brothel as a minstrel to earn some money. In the end, she was able to amass enough money to send him to the capital.

Later, when the husband passed the exam and became an official, his wife was ecstatic and knew that she had done the right thing. It was not long before her husband's colleagues found out that she had worked in a brothel. Afraid of bringing dishonor and shame to her husband, this woman sacrificed her life in the end. She leapt to her death from Wife-Yearning Cliff so no shame would befall her husband.

Their story should have ended there. The husband would grow wealthy in his new position, and with the brothel and his wife no longer an issue, he could marry again. Perhaps he would be too ashamed to even mention her.

But this wife had underestimated the love her husband had for her!

Upon hearing the news of her death, her husband was filled with sadness. He stayed by the cliff day and night, without eating or sleeping, hoping to catch a glimpse of her spirit, longing that her spirit would return to unite with him, but…

One day passed, two day passed… fifteen days passed!

The official could have enjoyed a luxurious life, but died on the cliff instead.

To commemorate the wife who sacrificed all for her husband, and the husband whose undying love touched many, people dubbed the place "Wife-Yearning Cliff".

A tragic story, with a tragic ending, will always remain unforgettable.

Sadly, many years have passed, and there stood the grave of Madame

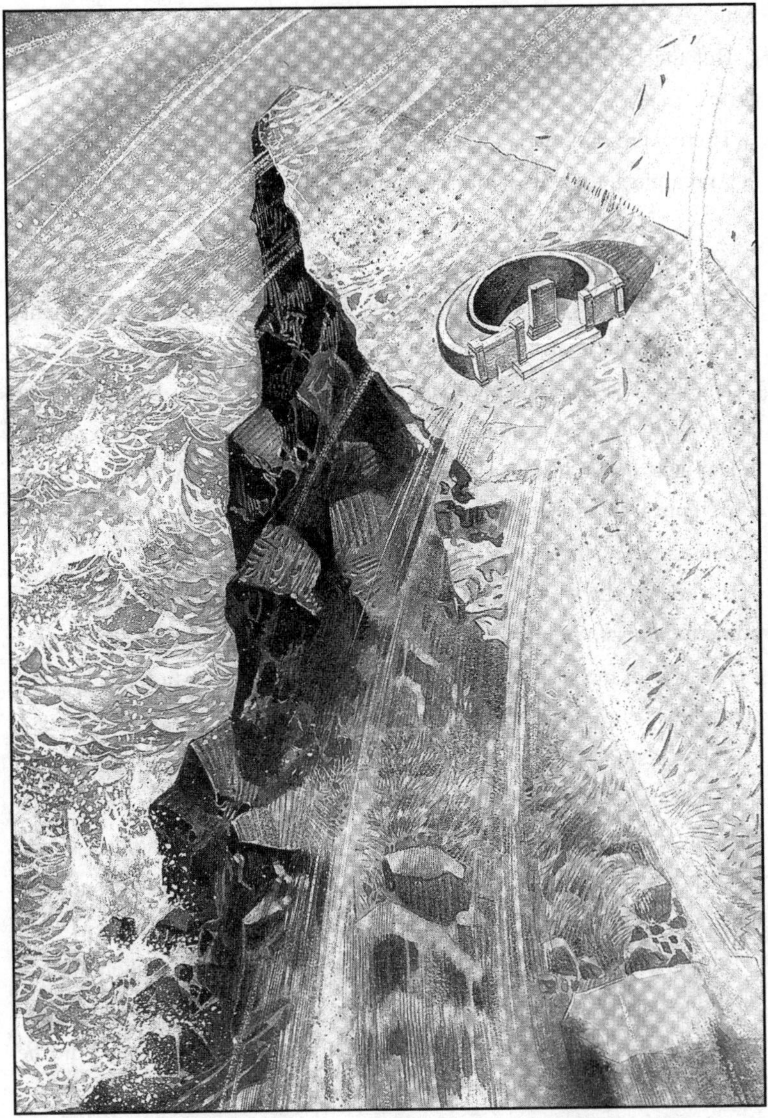

Mu…

But the husband, Mu Long didn't come despite his yearning for his wife!

There were only two sons who yearned for their mother.

And a niece that yearns for her aunt!


After half a day of walking, Ying Ming, Hiro and Xiao Yu finally arrived at Wife Yearning Cliff.

Twilight was approaching, and if it was not for Chiu Hong delaying their departure, they would have arrived much earlier.

Daylight began to fade. Under the last rays of the sun, Wife-Yearning Cliff appeared especially sorrowful. Madame Mu's grave on the cliff appeared especially lonely.

But today, she was no longer alone. Her two most treasured sons had come together to pray for her and visit her.

They all lit incense in her honor. And while the three lit incense at the same time, they stood far apart from one another.

Xiao Yu stood between Hiro and Ying Ming, separating them. She did not want to do so, but Hiro always seemed to look down on Ying Ming, and Ying Ming always avoided Hiro -- as if afraid that his bad luck would kill off Madame Mu's only remaining son. He believed that his "lone star" luck had killed Madame Mu, and did not want to risk her only son as well.

Actually, he kept a distance from everyone when he could help it.

On the way, Ying Ming did not speak to either Xiao Yu or Hiro, carrying on as if alone. For Hiro, this mattered very little; not once did he glance at Ying Ming, as if Ying Ming didn't even exist.

During the past five years, Hiro had been using every and any opportunity, no matter how small, to openly humiliate and degrade Ying Ming.

When Hiro wanted to go out, he would asked Ying Ming to prep and groom the horse for him, otherwise he wouldn't allow him to stay in Castle Mu. Even worse, Hiro picked the dirtiest horse in the stable, and asked Ying Ming to clean it from head to tail! It was the type of work reserved for the lowliest of servants in the Castle. This is how Hiro treated Ying Ming.

That's not all, when he climbed atop the horse that Ying Ming had spent all night preparing, he even kicked Ying Ming, opening a gash in his head. He truly hated Ying Ming.

But was his anger towards Ying Ming really caused by his mother's death? Is he really that kind of a person?

Mu Long was even worse! He didn't even treat Ying Ming as a person. Whenever he crossed Ying Ming's path in the Castle, he wouldn't even twitch a muscle of recognition.

Even so, Ying Ming acted as if he owed the father and son everything. No matter how terribly they treated him, he just took it all without a single gripe.

In this big, wide world, there are plenty of places for a young man to go. The question remained why did he stay in Castle Mu? Why did he continue to subject himself to such abuse?

Perhaps he cannot let go.

Mu Long is, after all, his father -- a father that bought him for five taels of silver. Although his methods were unsavory, he still put down cold, hard money and took him away from his drunken loser of a father, raising him all these years.

He also couldn't let go of an older brother, a brother that never cared for him, and even began to hate him after their mother's death. If he could continue to care for Madame Mu's family, then he would feel his life was worthwhile.

So every night, when Mu Long was once again asleep at his desk, a pair of silent hands would act as Madame Mu had done so long ago, and with devoted heart, put a cape over him…

Every morning Hiro would find a heated pan of water for him to wash his face. This pan of heated water was originally from Madame Mu…

But Hiro had quickly figured out who was responsible for the water. He never used it, and whenever Ying Ming passed by, he would deliberately pour the water out in front of him.

An open act of denial!

But his heart? Does it remain untouched?

Only Xiao Yu, as an observer could see the situation more clearly. She has secretly witnessed all the things Ying Ming had done for them.

Although she did not approve of Hiro's attitude toward Ying Ming, she didn't blame him, because she knew how much he was hurt by his mother's death. It was no wonder that he hated Ying Ming. But maybe one day, he might come to forgive him.

She admired Ying Ming, perhaps because he was such a rare individual.

But sadly the light of swords had disappeared completely from his eyes, and it was this light that she admired most! And today in front aunt Mu's grave, she secretly prayed to Madame Mu.

"Auntie, please protect Brother Ying Ming. I hope that he will soon gain back the light that he lost, and I hope that you can protect the two brothers so that they will…"

She hesitated, glancing up at each of them. "…one day reconcile!"

This was Xiao Yu's most sincere and only wish. After praying, she inadvertently looked at Ying Ming standing to her right. He was deep in prayer, with his brow furrowed in concentration, a sense of sorrow increasing. Was he, like Xiao Yu, praying for the happiness of the Mu Family?

Then Xiao Yu glanced to Hiro standing to her left, and she was startled. Because Hiro stared dully at his mother's grave, his features like chiseled rock, as if silently telling his mother in heaven that he had no wishes or wants.

But he had a persistent and faithful heart to accomplish his mother's dying wish!

No matter what it took…

After praying to Madame Mu, the three of them began heading back. About half way to the market -- roughly 10 km from Castle Mu -- night quickly approached, and the market was crowded with people. Hiro and Xiao Yu seemed interested in the market, but Ying Ming was not. He did not seem to be interested in much at all, as if he could not fathom why he was still alive.

Just then in the crowded plaza, a strident voice rang out.

"Ha! I told you woman, there's no hope for your husband! You better just go and prepare for his funeral! Stop coming here to bother me!"

Hiro and Xiao Yu looked over in curiosity, but Ying Ming did not react. They too discovered a stall in the market place, where a man and a woman sat arguing. The woman must be the wife, and the man, looks to be about middle aged and blind. He must be the one who just spoke.

Looks like this blind man is a fortuneteller, nicknamed "Bone Teller".

The woman upon hearing the fortuneteller say that her husband is without hope, began to cry and plead.

"Sir! My husband is a kind man. He shouldn't be so… short-lived! And we have five sons and four daughters, if my husband were to die, how can a widow like me raise nine kids alone? Please, sir! I beg… I beg of you, please save my husband!"

The woman begged pitifully, her tears pouring. But the fortuneteller was unmoved; he just shook his head with abrupt rudeness.

"Hmph! I am known as the Bone Teller, and I have always predicted correctly, but do you think that I am some god? A year ago, your husband fell gravely ill and you came to ask me to do a bone telling, to see if your husband would survive. I told you then that your husband could not survive, and that you should just save the medical fees and let fate take its course! But you didn't listen to me! See! And now it's come to pass. The doctor even said that your husband would die in 10 days. Haha, it proves that I was right all along! Hey just go back and see your husband on his way! Stop annoying me!"

The Bone Teller was resolute in his cruelty, but the woman continued to plead.

"No! Sir! If I go back… it would just be to watch him die. So I will just kneel here in front of you, and beg you… Please tell me if there's any way to change fate, and save my husband! I would kneel here until I die…"

Xiao Yu's heart went out to this poor woman. There were so many unfortunate people in the world! Yet there were more people that were cold hearted, just like this Bone Teller…

The Bone Teller said coldly.

"Pah! Change fate? You must be dreaming! Let me tell you something! Fate cannot be changed! Your husband is going to die! It doesn't matter how long you kneel in front of me! I am blind anyway, so just go ahead and kneel there! But don't forget what I told you, your husband's fate cannot be changed! Hehe…"

Is fate really so immutable?

The fortune teller's words angered someone. A righteous someone!

Hiro!

Hiro surged through the crowd and proudly stood before the Bone Teller.

"Can fate really not be changed? You are a charlatan! How much do you know of fate? I think you're just a fraud cheating people out of their hard-earned money! My lady, how can you believe this man? Don't be sad!"

The Bone Teller felt good that someone had knelt and begged for his attention, but hearing a sixteen year old young boy ridicule him thus, angered him.

"Fool! What do you know? From the sound of your voice, you're only a child. When I started doing bone tellings, you weren't even born! Who are you to tell me what the will of heaven is or isn't?"

Xiao Yu was going to advise Hiro to stay calm before the Bone Teller's rudeness, but before she had a chance, he already spoke up.

"Hehe, you revealing heaven's will? Very good! Let's see how you reveal that!"

With that, Hiro put out his right hand and laughed wickedly.

"Old man! Why don't you try with my hand? If you can tell my past and future and convince me, then I will proclaim that you have the right to do as you please!"

"Hmph! Young punk!" The Bone Teller spoke up with confidence, "You think I'm scared of you? I am the real deal! All right! Let me see your hand! I will see what kind of trash you are?"

The two of them escalated the situation to a standstill! The Bone Teller grasped hold of Hiro's hand and became quite shocked at the touch of his palm!

Even with his half century of experience, he could never have fathomed this!

The hand he held had a very particular bone structure…

Seeing the Bone Teller's mystified face, Hiro laughed.

"See! Old man! You can't tell, can you! You're just fooling people here! And here you are telling people that 'Fate can't be changed!'? Now I've caught you!"

Strangely, the fortune teller did not argue. Concentration lined his face, as if he held the hand of the emperor.

"You… you're not human!" he exclaimed with shock.

Hiro laughed again.

"I think you've gone crazy, old man! If I'm not human, then what am I, a ghost?"

"No!" The Bone Teller said. "You're not a ghost, but you're not human either! Your natural bone structure shows that you are proud and dominant. You are a dragon and a ruler!"

Ruler? This shocked even Hiro! He suddenly remembered when his mother mentioned the challenge with Sword Saint before her death.

Sword Saint described how he thought Hiro was a ruler of swords, even before his birth…

"Old man, what are you talking about? The emperor is sitting in his grand palace, this talk is blasphemous."

"No, no, no!" The Bone Teller shook his head urgently, "I have been doing bone telling for half my life, I have read hundreds of thousands of people, and I know that I am right! You must be a ruler! And when I think further upon it, your bones are sharp and hard, the shape is like that of a sword. It's very possible that you are a ruler of swords!"

Xiao Yu listening intently, could not help but be shocked because she also heard her aunt mention something about a ruler of swords before her death.

Even the ever-silent and nonplus Ying Ming seem moved.

The Bone Teller continued to press and prod Hiro's bones.

"From your bone structure, you are close to becoming the ruler! Perhaps in three years time…"

Three years? Hiro will be nineteen then? And Ying Ming will be nineteen as well? That is the appointed time of the duel with Sword Saint!

Hiro, Ying Ming and Xiao Yu stood mutely in shock. Hiro and Xiao Yu looked at each other with awe; they felt that the old man's words seemed truthful, he did have some skills.

The Bone Teller's empty eye sockets held a look of sympathy. Strange, isn't he blind? And he is so stubborn and rude, why this sudden change? Showing an expression of sympathy? He continued talking to Hiro.

"It's a shame! A shame! You are the ruler of swords; you are cold-hearted outside, but warm-hearted within. Although you act tough, you are sensitive to a fault. A promise has changed your entire life. And your life, because of this promise made to someone very close, will be forever changed! You have the fate of a ruler, but in the end, you are not fated to become one. It's really a shame..."

A promise to someone close? Hiro knew it was the promise he made to his mother about Ying Ming. Was this the promise that would alter his destiny, so that he would not become a ruler?

Hiro thought further, and lost his arrogant tone.

"Really? Because of a promise I made, I won't become a ruler? But if it is the wish of someone dear, if because of that I can not become a ruler, in the end I will fulfill the wish of the one dearest to me. Then it is worth it, right?"

The Bone Teller asked seriously, "Even if you sacrifice yourself, you won't regret it?"

Hiro didn't even have to think, and answered, "I won't regret it!"

"I admire that!" The bone teller hitched up his thumb, "You are a hero amongst men!"

What had been an argument just a moment ago had become an admirable understanding, and all the people gathered in the market place to look in wonder at them.

The Bone Teller stroked his long mustache.

"Extraordinary people have extraordinary bones and encounter many extraordinary events. I am so happy to have encountered such a rare specimen in my lifetime! Excuse me, young man, but are there any others in your party?"

Hiro didn't think that the Bone Teller would ask him such a question.

"I am here with my cousin and a waste of a person!" With that, he glared at Ying Ming.

The Bone Teller lifted his head.

"There is a saying, 'Things that are alike gather', an extraordinary person gathers other such people to him! Young man, I think that you are probably not the one with the extraordinary structure, can I try with your sister and the other?"

Hearing the Bone Teller's intentions to try Xiao Yu and Ying Ming, Hiro was about to refuse, but with a wicked smile he answered, "As you please! Because I want to test your theory and see how good you really are. I do not believe that fate cannot be changed! If you want to test two more people, it just gives me two more chances to prove that you are wrong!"

The Bone Teller only smiled. Hiro turned to Xiao Yu and said, "Sister Xiao Yu, if you don't mind, why don't you let the old man try?"

Xiao Yu heard the old Bone Teller's words and they seemed somewhat true. She wondered what he would say to her. She thought it seemed interesting, and timidly held out her hand. The Bone Teller grasped her hand and showed another sign of regret. "Dear girl," he sighed, "your hand is soft and almost boneless, someone with this type of bone structure is bound to be kind, and most likely a true beauty. But the structure also shows a lonely early life; perhaps some type of tragedy left you orphaned. Your mother must have passed away early, and your father, though a gentle man, also died quite young. But luckily fate has arranged someone for you. If your early life has been spent alone, heaven will send you a husband, a true hero!"

Hearing that her future husband would be a true hero, Xiao Yu's face turned bright red, and because of the words "Hero" she glanced furtively at Ying Ming. Hiro saw this glance, and for some reason, his heart felt pain.

Maybe because in the five years that have passed, he had developed a strong friendship and feelings for her…

But Hiro quickly calmed his feelings and took on a strong countenance. The Bone Teller had yet, it seemed, to have anything bad to say to Xiao Yu, and before he could say more, Hiro stepped in.

"That's enough, my sister is kind-hearted, and of course she will find a great husband! But I want to know about my foster brother."

He glanced harshly at Ying Ming. Hearing that, the always silently watching Ying Ming responded, "My fate is not good." He paused, looking away. "I don't want to know my fate."

He was just about to leave, but Hiro rushed in front of him and grasped his right hand.

"Hold it! I don't care if you don't want to know your fate!" He tightened his grip.

"I want to know!"

Yes, he really wanted to know how his fate linked with this foster brother's! Does he hope that Ying Ming's fate will be bad? Or perhaps he was not concerned for Ying Ming, and was only worried about his own fate?

Regardless of the reason, Hiro clamped down on Ying Ming's hand and brought it over to the Bone Teller. Ying Ming was shocked; he didn't think that Hiro would force him to do this. Although he's gone along with Madame Mu's wish for so long, and he lets them order him about, he was prepared to defy Hiro and rip his hand free.

With his eight different masters' teachings, Ying Ming thought he could easily break free, but no matter how he struggled, Hiro's hands were like an iron vise. He could not break free!

Looking at Ying Ming's look of shock, Hiro smiled wickedly.

"What? Are you really surprised? Remember, five years ago when you single-handedly broke eight swords? You were so heroic then! It's like you saved me! But times are different now! These past five years I have been studying and practicing the martial arts that father taught me. I've also been reading and researching other sword styles and martial arts, I am no longer that same boy five years ago! But you! These five years, I've watched you let yourself go. You didn't even practice, so what if you possess natural talent? It is nothing without hard work and practice, your skill level is the same as it was five years ago! I have already surpassed you! You are no longer worthy to be my opponent!"

Yes! Even a naturally talented hero means nothing. In this world, nothing great is accomplished without hard work! No matter who the person is, without diligence, they will amount to nothing in the end.

Surprisingly, Hiro is stronger, and Ying Ming could not resist. Hiro put Ying Ming's hand into the Bone Teller's hands. But when the Bone Teller touched Ying Ming's hands, his whole body shook! He also loudly screamed, "No. Impossible! Impossible! How can there be such a person in this world? No, not human... a monster? You are not human, not ghost, not god, not ruler! You are a monster that was born to use the sword! You are a lone, unlucky star! All those around you are doomed! Ahhh... How can there be such an ill-fated person in this world? You are a sword monster! Even if you become a hero, a leader, so what? The world will turn to ash because of you! It will lose all luster! Ahh! You... you're an evil monster, why don't you die already? Instead of living to bring harm to others? And killing all those close to you?"

The Bone Teller exclaimed with horror, throwing Ying Ming's hand aside, as if the lone star's bad luck would kill him if he held it a moment longer.

Unbelievably, that's how it ended! That's how it ended!

Ying Ming stood in shock. He's always known that his fate was bad, but the description of the Bone Teller was so horrific! As if his existence just meant the death of all those around him! Also the fear and revulsion shown by the Bone Teller was the same as that fortune teller so long ago. A mad fear!

Xiao Yu felt only sympathy for Ying Ming, because the Bone Teller said such horrible things about him in the middle of a crowd. The crowd stood shocked and Ying Ming had no esteem to speak of now, and what of his heart?

Hiro's heart ached with regret! He couldn't have predicted that it would end this way! Perhaps he thought the Bone Teller would have told him that he was a "Hero of all times" and thus encouraged Ying Ming. But who knew that the Bone Teller would say such terrible things.

Hiro tried to salvage the situation. Forcing a smile, he said, "Hehe! Kill all those around him and destroy the world? Bone Teller, I think that you've drank too much, or perhaps you're not as good as you claim! If you could really see what he looked like, you would know that he was merely a useless pile of trash.You're saying he's a monster that destroys all. I don't even think that he can kill a dog!"

Glancing sideways towards Ying Ming, Hiro continued, "Actually it doesn't matter if one is a terrible monster that causes destruction. What is important is to never bow down to fate! So what if it's fated, so what if it's destined? If someone believed that his life was preordained, he would naturally follow that path. But if that same person did not believe in fate, and fought against the unfair fate given to him, then he could possibly change his own fate. The future is not yet here, and he holds fate in his own hands!"

Yes! Fate is in one's own hands! This is Madame Mu's dying wish for Ying Ming! Now Hiro has said it again, even the Bone Teller is forced to agree! A sixteen year old young man spoke with the wisdom of a lifetime.

Hiro was afraid that Ying Mind did not understand what he meant, so he quickly added, "No matter what, no matter if you're good, evil, a god or a demon, can everything be perfect? As long as you've tried your best as a human being to truly live, then you can have a clean conscience! That is why I never believe in fate! I believe we control our own fate!"

Hiro's honest words spoke of his own belief, but were meant to incite Ying Ming. But Ying Ming listened without emotion, until finally he, in a seemingly regretful tone, spoke.

"Unfortunately, I don't have a clean conscience!"

His heart had been clouded forever by the tragic death of Madame Mu. His conscience had forever been stained.

That was why he had continued to stay in Castle Mu without any complaint. He just wanted to watch over the Mu family in her place.

Hiro was startled, and so was Xiao Yu. Hiro began to understand why Ying Ming had lost all his will, what more could he say? Just then, Ying Ming turned his back on the crowd and left!

"Brother Ying Ming!" Seeing his deathly demeanor, Xiao Yu worried what he would do, and hurried to follow. Hiro went along too, but before he stepped away, a small girl's voice called out.

"Excuse me, sir? I do not think that your adopted brother is a lone star!"

Hiro was startled, if these words were spoken by an adult it would not have been so interesting, but spoken by a small girl, it seemed overly mature. When he turned his head, he saw it was an eight year old girl standing behind him.

Although this girl was young, she had a face filled with wisdom. Her clothes looked old but tidy, and her hair was tied in a woman's bun. Her face was covered with dust from the road, and on her back was a short bow and a quiver full of arrows. On her waist was a small bag with the word "Phoenix" sewn on it.

Hiro already felt the girl's words were curious, and upon seeing her mature dress, he was even more intrigued. Hiro asked, "Little sister, you say that my adopted brother is not a lone star, why?"

The girl's eyes shone with the light of wisdom.

"His eyes look very sad, a complex sorrow, but there is no harm being directed outward, how can he be a lone star?"

It's incredible that a young girl could see through what so many adults missed! Hiro was filled with joy, he talked to her more.

"But that Bone Teller said that he is fated to be a lone star. It is not something that he can prevent himself..."

Before Hiro could finish, the little girl cut in.

"How can that be? That he cannot stop it himself? He has you! You are his big brother; you will surely find a way to help him!"

Hiro smiled.

"Me, help him? Hehe, little sister, did you not hear when I called him useless trash? Put him down? What makes you think I would help him?"

The small girl answered, "No! You're not putting him down! You're doing it for his own good."

Seeing that a small girl could understand the reasoning of a man, he felt his emotions stir. For the first time, he felt that there was someone who understood him in this world.

"For his... own good? Little sister, why do you say that?"

The girl answered, "I can 'feel' it! What people can 'see' is not necessarily the truth! Some things that you cannot see, but instead 'feel' are the real truth!"

"She looked at him with knowing eyes and continued. "Sir, although you seem very proud and arrogant, you have very kind eyes! Especially when you look at your adopted brother, you seem angry, but you are actually not, you're doing it for his own good."

Looks angry, but is actually not? This little girl has such a wise view? Hiro felt more interested, the girl spoke up again, "You're doing it for his benefit, but he is doing his best for you as well! Sir, your adopted brother's eyes seem very dark, almost without any luster. But I feel deep, deep down, the light is still there. He just hasn't shown it yet, and when he does, he will be a great hero!"

As the little girl spoke, her eyes were filled with admiration and adoration. Although Ying Ming had long left, she was still recalling his presence, a hero's presence!

Seeing the admiration on the young girl's face, Hiro was even happier. Because there was another girl who admired Ying Ming just as he did, and she was only a child. He spoke to her again, "You are an interesting little girl! Little sister, tell me, what is your name?"

The little girl seemed shy. Peeking at the satchel tied to her waist with the word "Phoenix", she started to reply.

"My last name is 'Phoenix', and first name is 'Dance'!"

Phoenix Dance? What a beautiful name! But Hiro could little imagine that one day this young girl would truly become a phoenix with her wings open at Ying Ming's side! That she would follow him her entire life as a faithful servant!

She admired him! Adored him! Protected him! Forgave him! Understood him! And even... love him!

Love without return, fate without fruition -- in the end they become not quite servant and master. This is Phoenix Dance...

This place is surrounded year round by heavy fog, green waters and a cold mountain. This is an ice mountain amidst the green waters!

Here reside two swords!

These swords are not made of any bronze, steel, gold or silver. In fact, the two swords are made of stone!

Are stone swords real swords?

No one knows who embedded these two swords on top of the ice mountain! The sword tips embedded into the earthy mantle!

From the dust and scars on the swords, they seemed to have been here since the beginning of time, through countless seasons, and many ages.

They are like two sentinels of justice, forever watching from atop the mountain, looking down upon the injustices of the world. They want to help, but cannot, because no one pulled them out to purge the injustices!

No! More accurately, no one *can* draw them out!

Never!

But in this desolate night, someone has come to the top of the ice mountain, to draw the swords!

The forty-two year old Sword Saint!

Sword Saint wasted no time! Leaping up and landing between the two swords, his right palm shot forth, towards one of the stone swords!

He never wastes any time! Because time is valuable even to an idiot, and for a saint it is even more precious! Time passes in the blink of an eye, or at the slow pace of a snail, but no one can stop the tides of time!

Sword Saint's hands reached towards the sword, and stop in midair. His whole body was suddenly stilled.

He stopped because as his hands neared the swords, a new crack appeared on the two swords, as if preparing to shatter and return to dust!

Why would the swords crack? Is it because that even though the swords are inanimate, they still have a will of their own? They do not welcome Sword Saint. Perhaps because he is merely a "Saint"!

He is not worthy!

So they cracked, showing that they would rather perish than be drawn by someone not suited, they would rather perish.

Cease to be!

This is the true mien of a hero! For the swords are like heroes!

Seeing the crack on the sword, Sword Saint's anger boils.

"Damn it! How dare you! Even Peerless Sword submitted to my undefeated hands, but you two ugly swords would rather break than submit? Why won't you allow me to draw you?"

"DAMN IT!"

With this insult, Sword Saint could no longer contain his anger, and screamed at the heavens! In rage!

At that moment, thunder roared, and a bolt of lightning struck down upon Sword Saint. Fortunately, Sword Saint's mighty skill allowed him to dodge!

Sword Saint clenched his fist. "Damn it!"

Having almost been struck by lightning, Sword Saint continued to rail at the heavens. Lifting up his Peerless Sword, he screamed at the skies.

"Heavens! You dare try to smite me? You DARE smite me?"

He waved his sword defiantly. "Who do you think you are? You are only the heavens! You are mute! You are deaf! You can't understand the suffering of mankind! You have no right to smite me! PAH!"

He lowered his sword and narrowed his eyes. "Heavens! Listen up! One day, I, Sword Saint shall surpass all others, and surpass you! Listen to me! There is nothing that I, Sword Saint, can not accomplish in this world. One day I will draw out these two swords that have humiliated me! And they shall be mine!"

He paused on his words. "Hero!"

Another dramatic pause. "Sword!"

Hero Sword? These two strange looking swords were called "Hero"?

Why will they not allow the powerful Sword Saint to draw them?

Who are they waiting for?

The two swords are silent. When Sword Saint called out their names, the thunder roared in the heavens once more, as if the heavens were giving Sword Saint a definite answer:

Though he was a saint, he was not...

A hero!

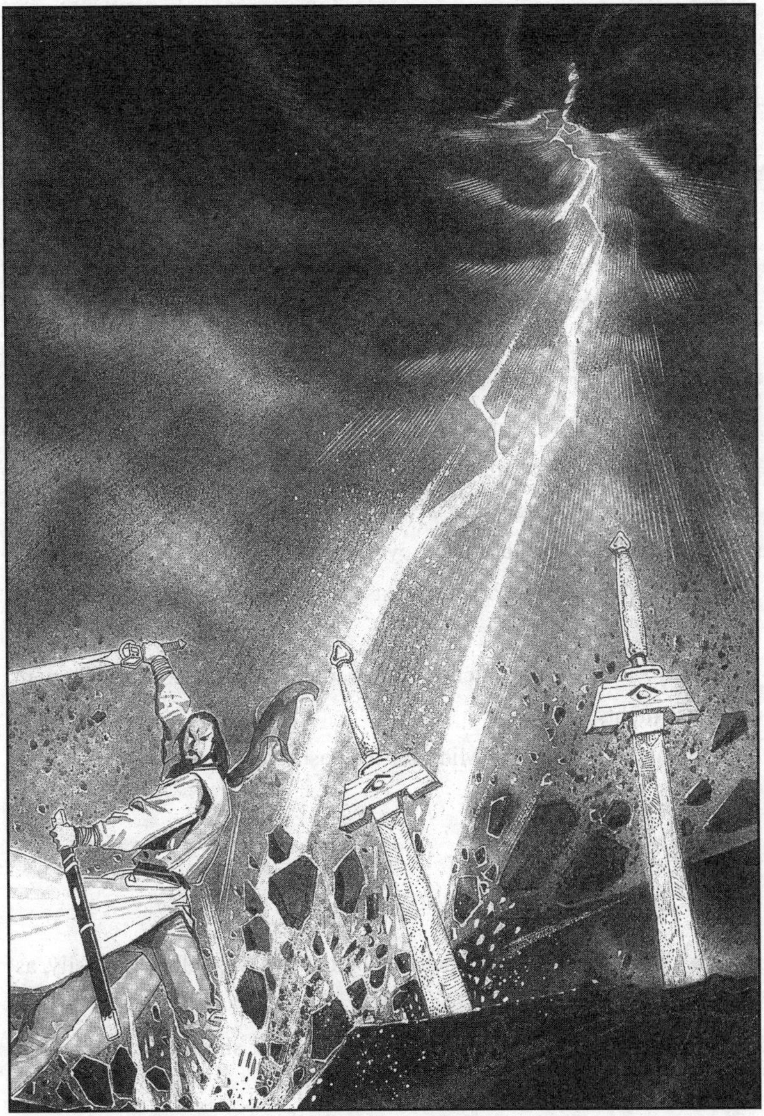

On another cliff of the ice mountain, two individuals watched the humiliation of Sword Saint. One was short, the other tall. One old and one young!

The long haired young man was shocked by Sword Saint's humiliation.

"Even Sword Saint is not good enough for those two swords?"

The elder one answered, "No, not good enough, even if he is a saint!"

"Then who is good enough for the swords? Who can draw them out?"

"Well, perhaps one of the two people I have seen!"

"Who are they?"

"No rush! You will know soon enough! Because..." the elder one paused slightly, "...they are already within my grasp!"

With that the elder glanced at the young man by his side. The pale moonlight reflected off the elder's eyes, glinting with the light of wisdom.

His eyes were filled with wisdom, as he watched the brothers these past five year!

It's him! These eyes watched, from countless dark corners, through countless nights...

Watching Hiro and Ying Ming for the past five years!

It's...

Him?


Outside the temple, the branches shook and leaves fell away easily, as if exhausted.

Inside the temple, the Buddha statues lost their sheen and luster, as if weary of shining brightly.

But, "he" was not yet tired.

Evening classes were long over, and the monks of the temple were readying themselves for sleep. Only a seventeen year old monk in white cassocks showed no sign of weariness. He continued his chanting and prayers.

Even the walls became tired of his voice.

But he was still not tired.

He continued until a barely audible sound broke his litany of prayers.

Footsteps!

He heard the steps come near, but did not turn. He continued concentrating on his prayers. Perhaps his heart had experienced too much sorrow and he needed his prayers to remain calm?

It was because he was a monk missing fifteen years of memory. Is he using the prayers to fill the emptiness in his mind?

The approaching figure seemed to understand the young monks need for prayer. He sighed.

"My student, although you chant the sutras, your heart shows that you do not understand them. You have been praying for ten days and nights without rest. It is useless to pray without reaching an understanding in your heart."

What? This white-robed monk has been praying for ten days and nights? This incredible will power marks him as extraordinary; yet if he is so extraordinary, why must he pray so hard?

The white-robed monk heard the words and stopped. After long moments, he finally sighed deeply.

"Master, you know why! Two years ago, you bade me to drink the 'Tea of Forgetfulness,' hoping that I would forget the tragedies of the past fifteen years. I have forgotten many things, but no matter what I do, I feel this strange sadness in my heart that I cannot erase, as if there is a story deep inside my heart, that I can never forget. That is why I pray so much. I hope to erase that sense of sorrow although I no longer know its cause. It is true, I do not understand the sutra I chant…"

The figure gave a futile smile.

"Ah, giving you the Tea of Forgetfulness was the one big mistake I, the Monk King, made. I thought the tea I brewed would be as good as the one given in Hades to make you forget your mortal life and start over anew. And the memory of the events was erased, but not the sorrow that they left behind?"

So this is the leader of the temple, Monk King, the very same one that Sword Saint visited many years ago!

Monk King looks a great deal older than he did ten years ago. His voice has turned slightly hoarse. Even the mighty Monk King can not escape the ravages of time.

Upon seeing the confusion in his pupil's face, the Monk King said, "But I have thought of a way to ease your sorrow."

The monk seems to brighten.

"Master, what is it?"

"Why not a thousand mile journey rather than a thousand dusty tomes!" the wise Monk King answered. "Just as ten years of prayer is not as good as one moment of enlightenment. My student, I want you to go complete a task for me. After you have completed this task, perhaps you will see through the sadness in your heart and reach enlightenment!"

"Master, what is this task?"

"It concerns 'him'!"

"Him? Master, do you mean that person you saw many years ago with your mirror? A person destined to live forever in sorrow?"

"Yes. I should really be the one to go, but I am getting on in years. I know the time of my passing is near. Perhaps in this very month…"

"Master, if that is true, then I can not go. How can I leave you behind at a time like this?"

The Monk King smiled, "My student, of course I understand how you feel in this matter. But we are on two different paths now. If my death were to tie you down, I would not be able to go contently into the after-life."

"Master, I still don't understand, if you say he is fated to be forever in sorrow, then what can be done about it?"

The Monk King smiled once again.

"It is a good thing that you do not yet understand! Since you do not understand, you will think upon it. When you think upon it, then one day you will understand it. When you understand it in its totality, then you will have found enlightenment!"

The Monk King's words showed his incredible wisdom and deep philosophical understanding of human nature.

Yet the seventeen year old monk was still worried for his master, he seemed to hesitate. The Monk King sighed.

"When it is time to eat, you should eat. When it is time to drink water, you should drink. When it is time to find answers, you should go!"

He paused and gestured with his hand. "One should do what is appropriate at the moment -- that is life!"

The Monk King lifted his head. "My student, after you've lost your fifteen years of memory, haven't you often asked me why so many events were foreordained? Why must it be up to fate? Why must there be a cycle of life and death, and so on?"

The young monk nodded gravely.

"Yes, I have never found that answer! If it is all up to destiny, if life is already preordained and human beings can not change their fate, then what is the use of living when we are all just pawns of the heavens? If one can do nothing of one's own free will, then what is the use of living? It seems meaningless..."

Seeing him sink once more into uncertainty, the Monk King quickly interjected, "That is the answer you must seek! My pupil, let me tell you. The answer you seek can be found with 'him'. You will understand what is meant by fate. Why one must live on, even if one cannot change fate."

"But, Master --"

"No more hesitation!" The Monk King waved his voluminous robes and led the white-robed monk outside the temple. Then with another wave of his arms, the ten foot high metal doors closed shut, separating student and master.

What incredible chi! He must be one of the top five martial artists in the land!

"My pupil, although you no longer remember the events of the past fifteen years, you still retain my teachings of 'Karma Reincarnation'. You are the most suited for this task; it would be a shame if you didn't go..."

"But..." the white-robed monk's answer was still a "but".

The Monk King admired his pupil's kind heart, yet thinking of his student's future, he had to speak further.

"My pupil, if you don't go, I will never leave this place. You will only make me die faster of starvation. Why do you want to hide in this temple? You will never find enlightenment, even if you pray here all your life!"

"My pupil, just go! Find the answers you seek living life! Go and see 'his' fate! I am sure you will find the truths you still do not understand there in his fate!"

The white-robed monk seemed to have more to say, but the sound of the Monk King's chanting could be heard from within the temple.

*Heaven and Earth are empty, life is within;*
*Power and Name are empty, victory and losses pass as the wind;*
*Wealth and Riches are empty, who can grasp those after death;*
*Master and Father are empty, we will not meet on the road to Hades...*

The clear chanting is a farewell song from a kind-hearted master to his unwilling pupil. Upon hearing, the white-robed monk understood his Master's heart and with no reason left, quietly turned and walked away.

He finally left.

The wind gently lifted the white-robed monk's clothes, lifting his white cassocks to reveal his silk undergarment. Sewn on the silks were two barely visible words -- they were his name:

Bushi, meaning "Without Falsehood".

There is an old Buddhist saying:

Transcend all pain, and truth is.

Truth truth...

Will the white-robed monk's journey alleviate all his pain?

And will he discover enlightenment?

\*　　　\*　　　\*

It has been one month since Hiro, Ying Ming and Xiao Yu visited Madame Mu's grave.

Xiao Yu thought that she'd fallen in love with a boy.

If she didn't love him, then why was she always worried about how he felt?

Leaving the Bone Teller's stall, Hiro and Xiao Yu trailed behind Ying Ming.

Hiro seemed sorry about forcing Ying Ming to have his fortune told by the Bone Teller. He did not speak to Ying Ming the entire way back, so Xiao Yu was definitely not going to say anything.

She was saddened that Ying Ming was publicly shamed in that manner, for it was so strange! It's not as if she had been the one humiliated by the Bone Teller, so why was it that she felt sad? Unless she was feeling for Ying Ming?

And Ying Ming was exceptionally quiet. He slowly walked forward, his face remaining emotionless. He never turned around once to look at Hiro or Xiao Yu. The depth of his mind was perhaps filled with the Bone Teller's words, words that stabbed right into his most troublesome weakness.

*You are not human, not ghost, not god, not ruler! You are a monster that was born to use the sword! You are a lone, unlucky star! All those around you, will be doomed! Ahhh... How can there be such a lone, ill-fated person in this world? You are a sword monster! Even if you become a hero, a leader, so what? The world will turn to ash because of you! It will lose all luster! Ahh! You... you're an evil monster, why don't you die already, instead of living to bring harm to others and killing all those close to you?*

These words deeply wounded Ying Ming, who had always blamed him-

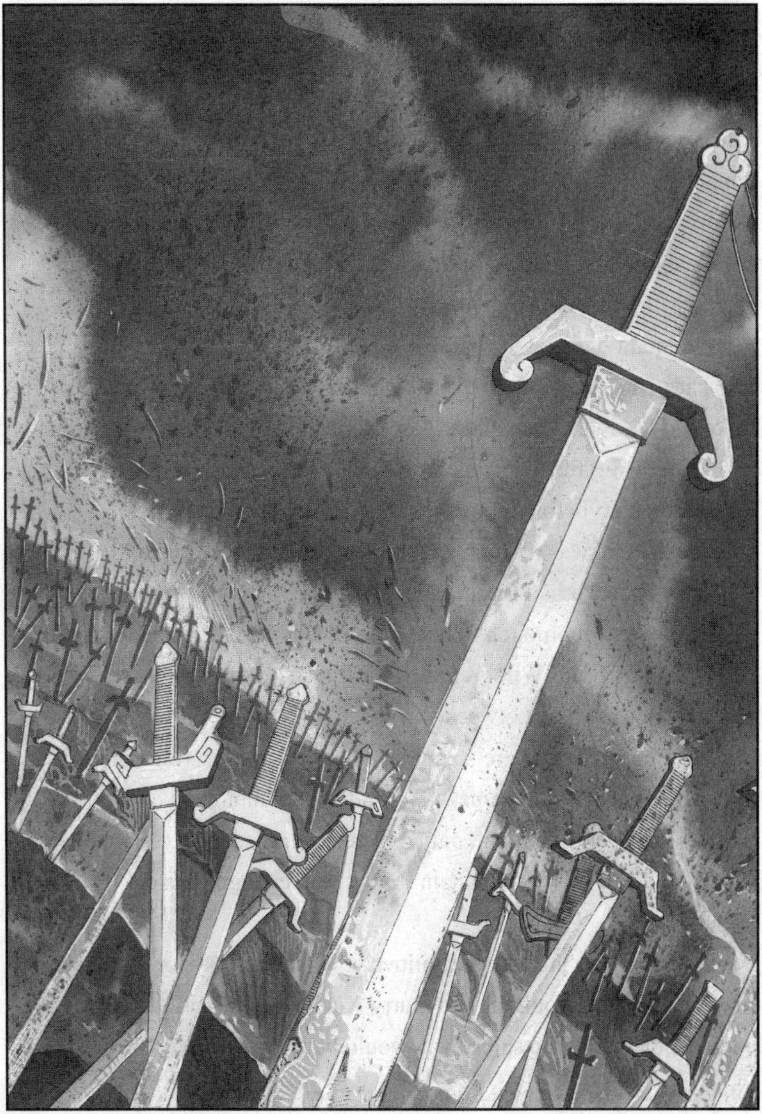

self for Madame Mu's death. His mind was a blank, he had no idea what he was doing or where he was going.

Numbly he walked toward Castle Mu. Hiro and Xiao Yu followed. After sometime, they found Ying Ming no longer walked forward; he had stopped.

Hiro and Xiao Yu lifted their heads to look at Ying Ming hoping that this meant he had gotten over his sadness, but it was because...

Ying Ming had no where to go!

A mountain blocked his path!

A path can often be blocked by hills. Yet when Xiao Yu and Hiro looked towards the mountain, they were mystified. Even the normally calm Ying Ming furrowed his brow.

The mountain before them should not be there!

Because there was no mountain on the way back to Castle Mu!

"Huh?" Xiao Yu had the strongest reaction.

"There was... no mountain here before. Did we take the wrong path?"

That's right! From Wife-Yearning Cliff back to Castle Mu, the passage leads through a valley between two sheer cliffs. This was where Xiao Yu, Hiro, and Ying Ming were standing. There was never a mountain in the valley! But today, from somewhere, suddenly a mountain appeared!

It was not a tall mountain, only a mere seventy to eighty feet in height, more like a hill than a mountain. Yet it was enough to block their path home.

With Hiro and Ying Ming's abilities, it would be easy for them to cross this hill. But they would have to carry Xiao Yu over, and that posed considerable dangers. The safest way would be for the three of them to walk around it.

How did this valley grow a mountain? It couldn't have fallen from the sky. Ying Ming appeared to have shaken off his earlier sullenness. Looking at the hill, he seemed to have gained some understanding.

"This is not a real mountain!"

"What?" Xiao Yu was secretly happy to hear him speak up, and quickly responded.

"Brother…Ying Ming, a mountain is a mountain, what makes it real or fake?"

Her question sounded slightly childish, but it was only because she was eager to get him to speak.

Before Ying Ming could answer, Hiro cut in.

"Cousin Xiao Yu, your eyes seem to be in working order, but you are not seeing! If you look closer, you will see that this is not a complete hill. It is pieced together with many large boulders!"

Xiao Yu looked towards the mountain, and just as Hiro described, she saw that the mountain was indeed made up of large boulders stacked carefully one on top of another. The edges were smooth and even, clearly cut by some sharp instrument.

Ying Ming looked towards the cliff face on either side of the valley. Seeing his look, Hiro spoke, "So scum, you noticed it too, huh?"

Hiro still felt bad about forcing Ying Ming to the Bone Teller, but it still didn't prevent him from humiliating Ying Ming at every opportunity.

Ying Ming did not turn, he stared intently at the tops of the cliffs.

"Brother Hiro, what did Ying Ming find?" Xiao Yu asked in curiosity.

Hiro answered, "If the scum and I are right, then this hill was made by a master swordsman. He cut away countless boulders with lightning speed; the falling rocks created this hill. It is all man made!"

Xiao Yu was awed.

"But, these rocks are huge! If a swordsman were really to have cut these boulders down, then, isn't this martial artist greater than the two of you?"

Hiro smiled with confidence.

"Not necessarily! I have been practicing our family's Palm style, plus my five years of sword studies, it would not be impossible for me to recreate this hill. That martial artist is not necessarily better than I am! But…"

He turned and glared at Ying Ming. "As for the trash that has been locking himself in, never striving for anything better, of course, I can not be placed in the same class as him!"

Hiro's words were clear in meaning, yet Ying Ming showed no emotion. In the past five years, he grew use to Hiro's constant degrading comments.

Xiao Yu didn't have the heart to see Hiro treat Ying Ming so poorly, so she quickly jumped in.

"But Brother Hiro, why did that martial artist place this here?"

Hiro responded, "Perhaps the person who created this hill wanted to prevent someone from going back to Castle Mu. Or perhaps, his target is the three of us!"

It was a bold conjecture, and Xiao Yu's heart pounded in fear, while Ying Ming silently agreed.

"Why would they want to stop us?" Xiao Yu couldn't help asking.

"Who knows?" Hiro answered. "They are forcing us to go around. It may be an ambush."

Xiao Yu became more and more worried as she listened.

"Brother Hiro, we can't go forward, and we can't go around… then what do we do?"

Hiro answered confidently, "I already know what I am going to do! Since they want us to go around, there must be something they want us to see. I am curious to find out as well, what kind of interesting things will happen!"

"As for you two…" Hiro looked towards Xiao Yu and Ying Ming, and laughed wickedly, "if you're not afraid, then come along! If you're afraid, hahaha! Then stay here and enjoy the long night! Though the nights are cold, it might be safer to stay. It's more suited for the cowardly! Hehe…" Hiro's words were intentionally meant to taunt, and with that he turned and walked around the hill.

Xiao Yu became more anxious; she turned towards Ying Ming and asked, "Brother Ying Ming, what should we do?"

Ying Ming walked past her and followed after the proud Hiro. Although Ying Ming kept his emotionless demeanor, he didn't forget to tell Xiao Yu.

"If you don't want to stay here alone, follow me!"

Normally he avoided everyone, even telling Xiao Yu that they were not so close five years ago. But from these words alone, it was clear that he cared about her.

Xiao Yu understood the meaning behind the words and smiled.

The three quickly skirted around the hill. After they left, shadows could be seen moving on the cliff side, two ominous shadows, one tall and one short.

Is it the same mysterious pair from the ice mountain?

Why are they here? Did they create the hill blocking the road?

A young man coldly looked down at Hiro and the group, and turned to the old man by his side.

"That's them?"

"Yes!" The old man answered. "It's that boy in white and the other one in black."

The young man showed signs of anger.

"Ha!" he began with a cold laugh. "That white clothed youth seems to be proud; his eyes are like twin swords that stab into an opponent's heart. I believe that his skill level and powers are similar to mine. I used five stances just now to create this hill, blocking their path, and I believe that that young man can do the same in five stances!"

The old man nodded, and looked towards Hiro with admiring eyes.

"True! You are my top student, and the best talent of the new generation in our clan. But that white clothed youth, I can detect a natural sword ruler's mien. Perhaps if he were to join our clan and understand the true ways of the sword, he might become an extraordinary swordsman!"

The young man's interest heightened.

"But are you sure, he is the legend of a hundred thousand years? -- the legend of the Heaven Sword?"

The old man did not answer, he thought for long moments, and answered cautiously, "It is likely so! Remember that night five years ago? I was staying at my brother's, five miles outside of Castle Mu, yet I felt a sword's chi disturbing the very heavens. A storm brewed, this sword chi was very much like our Sword Clan's legend of the Heavenly Sword. I followed that chi all the way to Castle Mu, and I found these two brothers..."

It was that stormy night five years ago. The night Ying Ming lifted up his head for the first time to Madame Mu. It was very likely that the legend of the heavenly sword the old man spoke of is not referring to Hiro, but rather Ying Ming.

But the old man did not know the truth, so he continued pondering.

"That night when I discovered the two brothers, that extraordinary sword chi had disappeared. Because the white clothed youth exudes a natural sword ruler's mien and he is a rare talent, I deeply believe he must be the legendary Heaven Sword. He just momentarily sheathed his sword chi…"

The young man interrupted his words with a reminder, "But don't forget, you found both brothers! That black clothed one can not be overlooked!"

The old man deeply believed in his own wisdom and judgment and smiled.

"It can't be him! That black clothed youth's eyes are filled with sorrow. I can not see through it to know his true potential. What is the highest level he can obtain? He is an unforgettable young man! But there isn't any sword chi about him! He has no will!"

The old man's words rang true; even if someone were a natural genius without the will to succeed or the determination to persevere, he would be wasting his talent -- wasting his life and amount to nothing.

But how would he know those moments before he arrived at Castle Mu, Ying Ming lifted up his head for the first time for Madame, and his sword chi stunned all. Even worse, Madame Mu's death had made him lose all will to become better in martial arts. The sword chi disappeared from him, and his sullen eyes became even duller, lacking any luster of life…

The young man by his side spoke once again.

"Although you think that black clothed youth lacks will, I have been observing his every move, and for some reason he seems to be standing higher than me, even higher than the sky. I have felt this chill in my heart, a premonition."

"What premonition?"

"Even if he is not the legendary Heaven Sword, he will become an enemy I must defeat!"

The old man laughed out loud, seeming even more entrenched in his beliefs, and said, "Hehe! You are my son, so be proud of your lineage. Don't give others so much credence. That black clothed youth does seem mysterious, but he lacks will and won't amount to anything! How can someone like that be a worthy opponent for my son!"

So these two are father and son? One is called Sword Wisdom, the other Sunder (Po Jun). Though they are father and son, they do not have the same last name, and what strange names!

That young man called Sunder doesn't seem to agree with his father, but not wanting to debate further, he changes the topic.

"No matter what, whoever becomes the legendary Heaven Sword, we will soon find out the truth."

The elder Sword Wisdom, nodded in agreement.

"Right, we created this obstacle to force them to go around. We are luring them there; when they arrive, 'Sword Spirit' will let us know if either is the true Heaven Sword."

"Also, they can help us retrieve something, because I will lead them to fight Sword Saint!"

These two have spent all this time creating this fake hill just to lead Hiro and Ying Ming to battle the legendary "Sword Saint"?

What is their purpose? What are they trying to gain from all this?

What is Sword Spirit?

\*　　　\*　　　\*

The mountain road was wild and meandering.

Twilight sank and grew dark as a forlorn lover's heart.

Night descended, but Hiro, Ying Ming and Xiao Yu continued traveling ahead.

They traversed around the hill, and Hiro could not have imagined how wide the valley was. It seemed endless, and the three traveled for quite sometime until twilight turned to night.

Hiro and Ying Ming thought that they would encounter something interesting, but nothing strange happened. There were no signs of habitation, only the heavy oppressive forest by their side.

In the gathering darkness, Xiao Yu unconsciously walked near Ying Ming. She couldn't understand why she was drawn to him more. She grew up with both Ying Ming and Hiro, and even spent more time with Hiro, yet she always wanted to be closer to Ying Ming, just like now.

Deep in her heart was there a seed of love, drawing her closer to Ying Ming? She feels something towards him…

The Bone Teller had already predicted she would gain her fondest wish: she would marry a "true hero".

Thinking such thoughts made Xiao Yu's heart flutter. She glanced towards Ying Ming and dared not think any further on it.

The three continued to walk around the valley, and as the night deepened, Xiao Yu turned to Hiro with worry consuming her face.

"Brother Hiro, we can't keep going like this. It's already so dark! There's no one around here. We might not be able to make it back to Castle Mu and we might not even find a place to spend the night!"

Hiro's face was full of confidence.

"Don't worry! Xiao Yu we are getting closer to what we were meant to see."

True, it was not far away. Right as Hiro answered, Ying Ming lifted his eyes!

There it was! A dreadful cry could be heard in the distance, like the cries of ghosts!

In the deep of night across a desolate valley, the sound of cries seemed more frightening. Xiao Yu was scared.

"Brother Hiro, those cries sound awful. Who would be crying here in the middle of nowhere? It doesn't even sound like one person, but more like a group!"

The cries came closer and clearer! There was definitely more than one person crying; at least a hundred cries sounded.

A hundred ghostly cries echoed through the night.

While Xiao Yu hesitated, Hiro and Ying Ming quickened their pace ahead towards the sounds.

Xiao Yu, afraid of being left behind, followed closely.

Shortly they arrived near the sound of the cries to discover that Xiao Yu's guess was completely wrong!

There were no ghosts crying in the night!

There was not even a single person about!

Hiro, Ying Ming and Xiao Yu looked intently into the distance and discovered the source of the hundred ghost cries!

In the darkness, there was an ominous mountain reaching high into the clouds. At the foot of the mountain stood countless swords!

No two swords were alike, some short, some long -- every style of

58

sword could be found there.

There were hundreds upon thousands of swords there, like some army of heroes gathered from across the land. Though various in design and origin all the swords shared two commonalities. They were each embedded inches into the ground and were stained and rusted.

The wailing came in from the night wind blowing across the field of swords. It seemed like the thousand swords were crying out in unison to the dead, dark night...

But why were these swords crying?

Xiao Yu finally understood the source of the cries, yet seeing these swords like a thousand corpses in a graveyard, only made her more afraid.

"Brother Hiro, why... are all these swords here? It seems so strange, even worse than a graveyard. Why don't we hurry and leave this place."

Hiro looked towards Ying Ming and found not a sense of fear on his brother, but sorrow for this graveyard of swords. Hiro was immediately interested.

"No hurry!" Hiro said, "Someone wanted us to see this. I'm sure that something interesting will happen now and --"

Before he finished speaking, a loud voice sounded behind them.

"You guess wrong! Nothing interesting will ever happen here! This is a graveyard for swords! The Grave of a Thousand Swords!"

The voice was powerful and masculine; he must be a great martial artist! Hiro, Ying Ming and Xiao Yu turned to find a bright light.

Their eyes lit up! The speaker was a tall man clad in armor of gold!

His hole body was shining like a golden dragon!

Not only was he wearing armor of gold, but he also held a giant golden sword with a fierce dragon carved on it. The speaker looked to be

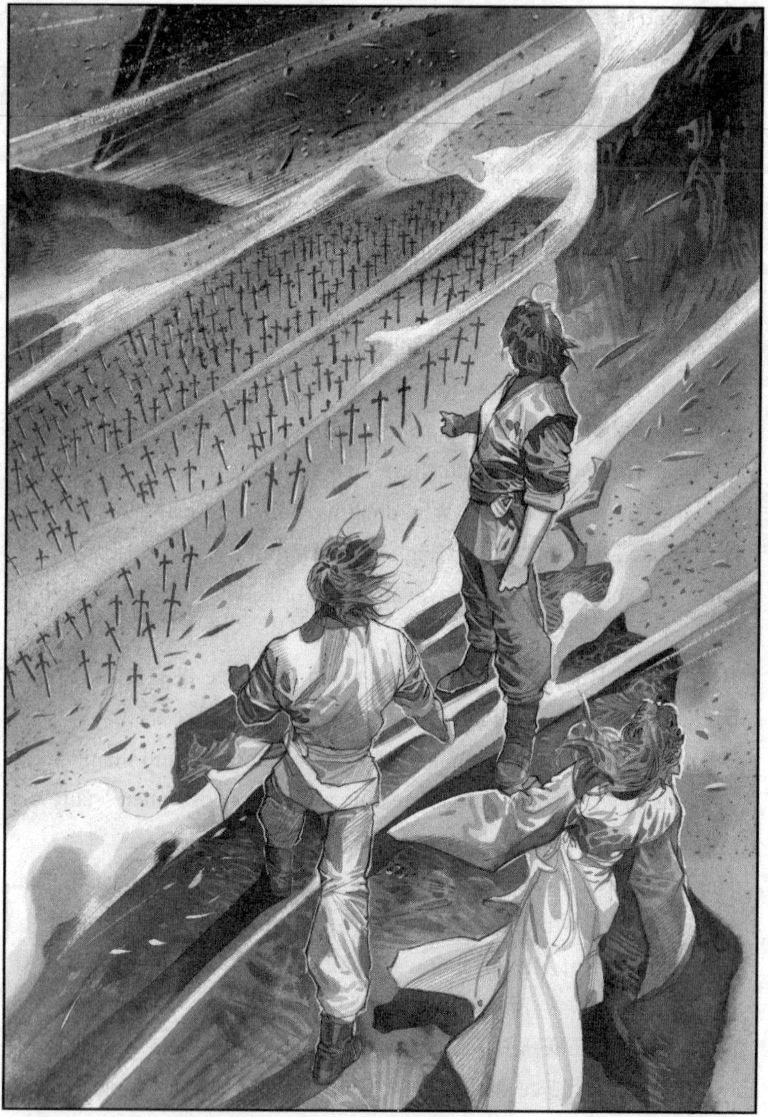

about thirty years of age, and appeared strong and powerful!

Behind the golden dragon man stood a short and stout individual. He was strong as a mountain, and covered with the skin of a tiger. He held a giant silver sword, and the image of a tiger was carved onto the hilt.

Seeing these two muscular men, Xiao Yu became more fearful. Ying Ming stood unmoving. Hiro took his time and observed the two men; he turned his mouth up in distaste.

"Hehe, my guess was right! Before anything interesting happened, we've already met two interesting looking people!"

The golden dragon man looked at the smiling Hiro and answered seriously, "Young fool! You have a sharp tongue! I shall introduce myself! My name is 'Sword Dragon'! Behind me is my second brother, 'Sword Tiger'! They call us 'Dragon Tiger Sword Pair'!"

Hiro continued to laugh.

"So that's why! It's Sword Dragon and Sword Tiger! No wonder your sword hilts are carved with a dragon and tiger, it's a match made in heaven. A big happy animal family!"

The golden armored man roared in anger at Hiro's condescending tone.

"You want to die! How dare you mock me! I will kill you with one strike!"

He lifted his sword, preparing to strike Hiro, but was stopped by Sword Tiger.

"Big brother, don't be provoked! This punk looks to be about sixteen; we don't need to worry about him! There are still things we need to do here, so we can't waste time with him!"

Although Sword Tiger looked to be a few years younger than his older brother, he seemed more experienced and rational. He clearly looked down on Hiro, Ying Ming and Xiao Yu. He viewed them as inexperienced martial artists, not worthy of his time!

Hiro responded with a laugh.

"Don't want to waste time? What's so important? I think that you are just a bunch of fools, pretending to be on some mighty errand!"

Of course, Hiro was not being truthful! From their stance, chi, and bearing, Sword Dragon and Sword Tiger were clearly mighty warriors! Yet Hiro had always been prideful, and could never stand down to anyone.

His taunt angered Sword Tiger this time.

"How dare you!" Sword Tiger bellowed. "All right, let me tell you something; the place you now stand is called 'Sword Grave'! The foot of this mountain is the starting point of 'Sword Peak'. We were planning to climb Sword Peak but now we find three children here, so we wanted to see what you were up to!"

Upon hearing "Sword Grave", and "Sword Peak", Hiro's brows knitted and even Ying Ming seemed deep in thought.

"What is this Sword Grave, Sword Peak?" Hiro asked. "Why do they both have Sword in their names? What is this place?"

"Haha! Fool, you know nothing. Everyone knows about this place. Sword Grave is the place where all swordsmen leave their swords when they climb Sword Peak! Over time the increasing abandoned swords left here grew so numerous it became known as Sword Grave!"

Hiro was even more curious.

"Why do swordsmen want to climb 'Sword Peak'? Why do they have to put their swords here before they climb up?"

Sword Dragon answered, "Because they seek that which resides on Sword Peak. To show their sincerity, they put their favored sword here."

"A swordsman should never part from his sword! What is on top of Sword Peak? What would make these swordsmen leave behind their beloved swords?"

Sword Tiger cut in, "Hehe! Of course, it is something extraordinary! Punks, if I tell you what it is, don't get too scared! At the peak is something swordsmen have sought through the ages… the 'Hero Sword'!"

Hero Sword?

These words made Hiro and Ying Ming shutter. Only Xiao Yu did not react.

Hiro and Ying Ming glanced at one another. They felt that they had heard of this name before. At the same time, blood coursed through their veins, and their hearts pumped faster.

It was a mystical feeling! The words "Hero Sword"seemed to link the two somehow -- it seemed fated that they would become entranced by it.

Perhaps, long ago, the Hero Sword had already been fated to meet the two brothers…

Sword Dragon seeing Hiro and Ying Ming in shock misunderstood their reactions.

"See, punks? You're fearful of the name. Wait until you see the sword!"

Hiro forced down the strong emotions evoked by Hero Sword, and asked, "There are hundreds upon thousands of rusted swords here. Does that mean that many swordsmen have come? Why don't they take their beloved swords with them when they leave? Is it because none came back alive?"

"No!" answered Sword Tiger, "It's just the opposite! All the swordsmen survived! However, after seeing Hero Sword, they felt that it was the most perfect and desirable sword in existence. All other swords became noth-

ing in comparison. A mere glance at Hero Sword, and they lost all interest in their own swords. If they can't have the Hero Sword, then they will
wield no other! This place became the Graveyard of a Thousand Swords
abandoned by their masters."

So that's why! Hiro and Xiao Yu looked towards the swords with a new
understanding. These swords must have seen some glorious days in the
hands of their wielder. They faithfully followed their masters into battle,
but in the end their masters fell in love with the Hero Sword and they
were tragically abandoned. If these swords were alive, perhaps they
would be filled with endless regret and sorrow…

Ying Ming's eyes filled with great sorrow for these rusted swords.

The Hero Sword was charismatic enough to make all these swordsmen
relinquish their beloved swords. Hiro could not begin to imagine its powers.

"This Hero Sword," Hiro began, bewildered, "is pretty powerful to
make all these swordsmen fall under its spell. But what is really so great
about it? Why does one sword attract so many?"

"You're wrong!" Sword Tiger corrected him. "The Hero Sword is not
one, but two swords!"

This was beyond Hiro and Ying Ming's wildest expectations, and Hiro
asked, "What? There are two Hero Swords? It is called 'Hero', and should
be peerless, how could there be more than one?"

Sword Tiger and Sword Dragon looked at one another, and then turned
condescending eyes at Hiro because he didn't know. Sword Tiger laughed
out loud.

"Fool! I told you, you don't know anything! For several hundred years,
atop Sword Peak, there has always been two Hero Swords, like two

brothers they are always together. These two Hero Swords are the same, waiting for their masters to claim them!"

Sword Dragon added, "It's true, the origins of these two swords are the same, and they originate in the legend of the 'Way of the Sword'."

"What legend?" Hiro asked.

Sword Tiger spoke each word succinctly, "Legend of the Heaven Sword!"

Legend of the Heaven Sword?

Both Hiro and Ying Ming reacted to the words 'Heaven Sword'. Their reactions were stronger than when they heard the words Hero Sword. Their hearts rang out, as if there was some emerging destiny awaiting them, linking their hearts, their fates…

Heaven Sword? What kind of sword was that? Or is it referring to *someone*?

Brothers Sword Dragon and Sword Tiger seemed more excited than anyone. They were planning to hike up the mountain to see the sword, but in the excitement of telling the Hero Sword tale, they forgot what they were doing.

So they told the tale of Heaven Sword.

This tale is about a person.

A sword master.

His name is...

Great Sword Master!

What is the origin of the Great Sword Master? Many origins are lost in antiquity, but this story starts with a young man, many ages ago.

At the time, the world was still young; there was no such thing as a "sword skill"...

The so called "sword" used by the people of the time, was merely a sharp implement in the vague shape of a sword. People just used the tool without any technique.

One day, in a particular village, a young man named "Master" began to change things.

This young man was especially wise and talented. He was revered by the entire village. But the young man was not satisfied, and liked to ponder questions that no one else thought of.

For example, he would ask the tribe elder why the swords were being waved around without any organization or discipline.

How does one decide to swing high or low?

Why not try to change the path of the sword swing to strike with additional power?

Why not change it into a structured "stance"?

But the elders laughed at his eager questions! For them a swing was a swing, a stab was a stab, and a kill was a kill! The sword was meant to hack, and there was no technique to such a tool, so no need to think further upon it.

But Master didn't think so, and he began studying this tool called the sword. On one quiet night, the villagers awoke to a loud thunder!

Lightning had struck Master's home. Everyone rushed to look, and saw that Master had survived without a scratch!

He was practicing with his sword!

# Legend of the Great Sword Master

The villagers found that the way Master used the sword was different from how they moved with the weapon! His method seemed extremely powerful! A power that rang through the very heavens!

As Master was practicing his sword, a storm gathered and lightning flashed. His sword techniques shook the skies, because he had created the world's first --

"Sword Stance"!

The heavens rejoiced at the discovery. A sword was the king of all blades! And it had finally found its "tao"!

From then on, the sword mixed with its tao to create sword skills to rid the world of evil and injustice!

To commemorate Master creating the first Sword Stance, the villagers honored him by changing his name to "Great Sword Master". But he was not satisfied with just one sword stance. He continued to research the sword, and in a short span of ten years, developed various styles of sword stances, and created the first school of the sword - Sword Clan!

The Great Sword Master's most impressive achievement, aside from creating the first sword stance and its variations, was in understanding the true essence of the sword. He created an incredible sword technique called the "Nameless Sword Technique"!

If someone naturally fated with the way of swords were to learn this technique, they would be able to understand all other sword techniques they encountered within one or two stances and see its true essence. If a sword technique had ten stances, someone using the Nameless Sword Technique could deduce the eleventh stance, which was more power than all the previous ten!

The Nameless Sword Technique was created in the first half of the

Great Sword Master's life! But sadly, this Sword Technique could only be understood by those whose fate linked with the sword. It is useless to all others.

When the Great Sword Master created the Nameless Sword Technique, he was already thirty. He thought he had already contributed enough to mankind, and began to live a quiet life.

But as fate would have it, just as the Great Sword Master was about to retire, he discovered a Scroll of Foretelling!

The Scroll foretold of many events revealing something terrible to the Great Sword Master.

A great calamity would befall the land!

The scroll told of an island country bearing the sun symbol conspiring against the great land. They would invade....

They would rape its women and kill its men!

They would pull the fetuses from women's wombs!

Thousands of innocent people would be buried alive!

This small island country's attack on the land would bring in an army of eight nations.

The Great Sword Master was shocked! He was not a very superstitious man, but the events foretold had already come to pass. Just as he was paralyzed by indecision, he thought of an idea.

The best way to avert this possible disaster was to prevent it!

Even if the events in the scroll were never to occur, it would be a good thing to be prepared!

He decided to do this one last great deed for mankind!

According to the scroll, the disaster did not have a specific time it would begin, but it would come. If at the time there were a great hero to lead a group of "storm riders", they could stop the cold ambitions of the island nation and prevent this disaster.

The disaster could be averted once by the actions of that great hero and the "storm riders", but peace would only last for a few hundred years. After two dynasties, the island nation of the sun would rise up again and the army of eight nations would seek once again to conquer the great land! The land may be saved if another hero were to come forth…

It would be a good deed already to push the disaster back! The Great Sword Master began to create a sword for that yet unborn hero...

The Hero Sword!

In his thirtieth year, he found a desolate mountain of ice and began forging the Hero Sword!

According to legend, the Great Sword Master spent fifty years on the ice mountain forging the swords. He finally finished the swords in his eightieth year. For his land, he'd given his entire life and energy. He died alone.

He never regretted his choices, because he knew the fate of millions had been at stake!

After fifty years, the Hero Sword was shaped but not truly forged.

Initially, when the Great Sword Master began thinking about creating the Hero Sword, he thought for thirty years without finding a solution. He wanted to make the strongest, most unbreakable, most noble hero's sword!

But the heavens did not forsake him; he finally found a compound that was half stone and half metal! It had the appearance of stone, but after hundreds of years, a change occurred in the nature of the stone, and it was transformed into a strong, unbreakable metal!

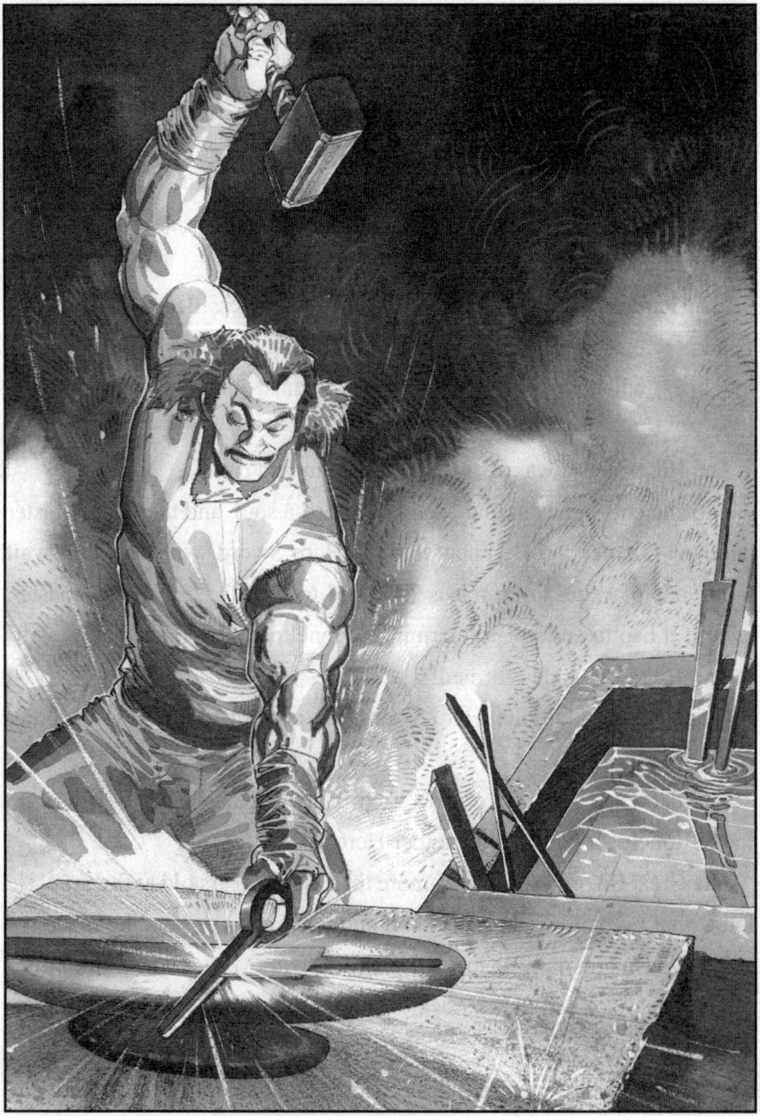

The Hero Sword was forged, but only by half. The outside of the metal was still stone, it would take hundreds of years more until the time was right for it to truly become a sword!

The Great Sword Master had finally accomplished his greatest deed; he embedded the sword into the top of the ice mountain. The sword tip turned jet black like a lonely, reluctant hero. The Great Sword Master finally understood.

"The hardest thing to overcome in life is loneliness! Hero Sword, don't you know that heroes are always fated to be alone? Your name is 'Hero'; loneliness will always be a part of you. You must endure this endless solitude…"

The Hero Sword was silent, and the tip turned darker.

The ancients believed that each sword had a soul, and the Great Master believed this deeply. He knew that the Hero Sword would have to wait thousands of years to be released. It had to wait for its rightful master, even if it had to endure an interminable loneliness. He looked at the leftover metal and an idea formed!

He made one additional Hero Sword, and embedded it next to the other Hero Sword!

The darkened Hero Sword reverted to its original luster -- it was no longer lonely! It had found another Hero!

The Great Sword Master was more than eighty years old at the time. He knew that his time was near an end and he would not be able to see the two Hero Swords take shape. The Great Sword Master was mortal after all; he could not live thousands of years.

He felt that his greatest deed was still incomplete. Using his Sword Fingers, he carved his Nameless Sword Techniques on the tips of the

Hero Swords and spoke solemnly to the two "heroes".

"Hero Swords, although you have each other for company, according to the Scroll of Foretelling there is only one true Hero! One Hero and one sword! You are destined to battle, and one of you will break! But I know that you won't regret, because you can spend your lifetime with a true companion and enjoy a genuine battle between good friends -- isn't it glorious?!

"But I hope that you will remember my words! No matter how long you have to wait, be true to your sword heart and soul. Only yield to someone worthy! Don't let someone unsuited pull you out! If someone were to forcibly pull you out, then you would rather shatter than be drawn!"

This is the Great Sword Master's only hope for the two swords. Although the swords could not speak, they both shone at once with a pale light, as if answering the Great Master, letting him know that they would await that hero and never yield to any other, be they God or Saint!

The Great Sword Master spoke again, "Good! My Hero Swords, you know I have given my life to your forging. I am not far from death, but I have this feeling, I feel that the hero who will draw you will be a sword, a 'Heaven Sword'…"

The Great Sword Master spoke with his last breath, "Heaven Sword!"

He had exhausted his strength, but his goodwill towards mankind made him go on. With his last breath, he spoke one last time.

"My… Nameless Sword Technique… it is useless to normal swordsmen. Only a heaven sword or someone with the natural talent of a heaven sword can understand it. Then the most suited person, if he were to obtain the unbreakable Hero Sword, plus my Nameless Technique, he would be the greatest hero of all time!"

With his last words spoken, the Great Sword Master passed away peacefully between the two Hero Swords!

Since that time, the two Hero swords have been atop the icy tip of Sword Peak, waiting for their rightful master to appear. No matter how long, they would wait…

But something strange happened!

When the legend of the Heaven Sword and the Hero Sword spread, people began to covet the Great Sword Master's Nameless Sword Technique. They climbed Sword Peak hoping to pull out the two Hero Swords for themselves, but the swords would always crack!

The two Hero Swords have a sword heart and soul that awaits their true master. They would rather shatter than be drawn by someone else!

After many years, more and more swordsmen have come to the mountain, and more and more swordsmen have failed. They are greedy, yet they respect the Hero Sword, so they leave their swords by the foot of the mountain. But no one has dared test if the swords will truly shatter, taking Nameless Sword technique with them into obscurity.

The two Hero Swords wait endlessly. No one knew when they would become true Hero Swords. The two lonely heroes, when will their masters come?

Who are the masters of the Hero Swords?

"Yes! Who are the masters of the Hero Swords?"

Hiro, Ying Ming and Xiao Yu listened intently to the story of the Great Sword Master, and they were touched by his heart. Hiro couldn't help but ask the question on everyone's mind.

"Of course!" Sword Dragon answered. "The two masters of the two Hero Swords are my brother and I!"

Sword Tiger agreed, "That's right! We will each get one Hero Sword, and then we will learn the Nameless Sword Technique. We will become invincible then! Hahaha…"

Hiro interrupted their dreaming.

"Don't use the Hero Swords and Nameless Sword Techniques for conquest. That is not what the Great Sword Master intended. That is not what he had in mind for a hero!"

Sword Dragon and Sword Tiger's faces stiffened, but Sword Dragon spoke up first.

"Damn it! Punk, I think you're asking to die! How dare you imply that we're not heroes?"

He struck out with his fist towards Hiro, but Sword Tiger stopped him.

"Big Brother, don't be so hasty. I see that punk has something planned. It's as if he already had someone in mind! Let's see who he thinks is a real hero!"

"You're right brother! Punk, if you don't think we're heroes, then who do you think is a hero?"

Hiro smiled lightly and looked at Ying Ming from the corner of his eyes, as if he already knew. But he didn't say anything and did not directly answer the question.

"Of course," he said, "I have someone in mind already! But I don't need to tell you."

"Ha!" Sword Tiger retorted. "You don't have an answer do you, probably because you don't even have anyone in mind! Of course, who could be more heroic than my brother and I? Unless…"

Sword Tiger's eyes turned towards the silently listening Ying Ming.

"Ha! Unless you think the boy following you like a dog would be a better hero than my brother and I? Haha…"

Sword Dragon and Sword Tiger began laughing uproariously.

Ying Ming didn't say anything, but trouble always had a way of getting him. Xiao Yu felt that the insult was not justified, and even Hiro showed a hint of anger. The carefree smile disappeared from his face, and seriously he said, "He is not my follower! He is my brother! Although I consider him trash, I will not allow others to insult him! Because only I can insult him! He owes me!"

Sword Tiger and Sword Dragon stood in shock, even Xiao Yu and Ying Ming were shocked!

Hiro looked like a proud eagle, able to soar across the skies, but remained behind to protect a younger brother that he wished could soar along by his side! He's waiting for another eagle to roam the skies! He is waiting patiently!

Seeing Hiro so serious, Sword Tiger lost interest in making fun of them, and turned towards his brother Sword Dragon and said, "Come on brother, it's getting late! We've been wasting our time with these punks! Let's hurry to the top of the mountain for the swords!"

Sword Dragon replied, "Sounds good! The Hero Swords are ours anyway! Even if I can't have them, I can at least grip it in my hand once. I don't care if they shatter! The sooner we get them, the sooner we can show up these young punks! We'll show them real heroes! Haha…"

With that Sword Dragon and Sword Tiger gave Hiro and Ying Ming one more look, then turned and leapt toward the top of the mountain!

But they didn't leave their swords behind in the Sword Grave!

Have they no respect for the Hero Swords? They think they can still draw Hero Sword while retaining their original swords?

Or perhaps it is because they are afraid to leave their expensive swords behind. Their gold Dragon Sword and silver Tiger Sword are extremely precious. Perhaps they believe Hiro and his group might want to steal them.

The two of them think Hiro, Ying Ming and Xiao Yu are no better than common thieves. Of course, Hiro knew what they thought. He was instantly filled with anger, he punched out towards the side of the mountain and with a loud boom a foot wide hole appeared on the cliff face!

Xiao Yu and Ying Ming have never seen Hiro so upset, and filled with worry. Xiao Yu asked, "Brother Hiro…"

Before she could even finish, Hiro announced, "Let's go!"

"Where?" Xiao Yu asked.

"Up!"

"What? Up? Brother Hiro, it looks really dangerous up there, I don't think we should annoy Sword Tiger and Sword Dragon anymore!"

Hiro didn't bother to answer the question, he just glanced towards Ying Ming and asked coldly, "The Hero Sword is a weapon of righteousness; I would like to see it! I also don't want those two idiot brothers to get anywhere near it, they are not worthy! They would forcibly take the swords and cause them to shatter! I have to stop them! Are you coming?"

Ying Ming didn't speak, but he already began walking towards the top of the mountain!

He answered with his actions!

Although he didn't want to improve his martial arts and he did not covet the Hero Sword, he did not want to see the Great Sword Master's grand dream of saving the land and its people destroyed by those two despicable brothers.

He felt that he should go!

As Hiro, Ying Ming and Xiao Yu left for the top of the mountain, two shadows appeared where they stood moments ago. Looking closely, it was one older and one younger man. It was Sword Wisdom and Sunder!

The young man named Sunder spoke, "Father, you guessed right! We lured them here with that makeshift hill. They will surely climb to Sword Peak now!"

Sword Wisdom nodded.

"Yes! When they climb to the top of Sword Peak and near the Hero Swords, we will know if they are the fated Heaven Swords. If they can really pull the Hero Swords out, then our mission can be accomplished..."

"But father," Sunder continued, "don't forget that Sword Saint is waiting up there. Do you really think they'll get to the Hero Swords with Sword Saint there?"

Sword Wisdom smiled and shook his head.

"I don't know the answer to that question. But I deeply believe that something interesting will happen when they meet up with Sword Saint! Let's hurry so we don't miss all the fun! Haha..."

The two laughed and began climbing the mountain, but there were more involved in this affair than even these two knew about.

As they climbed up the hill, there was someone else watching them. Ten yards outside of the Sword Grave, in a darkened corner...

A man in white!

More accurately, a seventeen year old monk in white cassocks!

It's him! He's finally done as his Master wished -- he's come to see that destiny!

With an expressionless face, he lifted his head toward the highest peaks of the tall mountain, and said softly, "They are finally nearing their true destiny."

"But these two strong and righteous men, why are they burdened with this horrible fate?"

"Master, if you have already seen with your Mirror that they can not change their fates, then why do you want me to observe them? What will I learn from their lives?"

Strange.

It was a very strange feeling.

As they neared "Sword Peak", Hiro and Ying Ming's hearts both experienced a very strange feeling.

They were still miles from the top of the peak, but at the same time, their hearts were suddenly assaulted by this strange feeling!

The feeling was so strange, because it was so complex!

How could it be described? Hiro and Ying Ming felt that there were two forces pulling them towards the mountaintop, ushering them towards some meeting. At the same time, the two felt that there was an even stronger force on Sword Peak warning them to stay away at all cost!

This stronger force was like that of an impossibly irresistible and dangerous foe!

Xiao Yu knew no martial arts, so she was not as susceptible to these forces; but even she could feel the mysterious pressure and suspense!

"Um…" Xiao Yu spoke up, "Brother Hiro, Brother Ying Ming, do you feel something? Like some force pressing down? It feels like… it's crowded here, but I don't see anything."

Ying Ming answered, "It is chi."

"Chi?" Xiao Yu didn't understand.

"Yes!" With a smile Hiro cut in, "It is a very dangerous type of chi -- the chi of a dangerous swordsman!"

With that, Hiro lifted up his right palm towards a falling leaf. With a loud rip, that withered leaf tore through Hiro's sleeve!

"Ah!" Xiao Yu was frightened, "It's just a leaf! How could it cut through your sleeve thus? Brother Hiro, how is this possible? Have my eyes gone bad?"

"No!" Hiro glanced towards Ying Ming, and then back to Xiao Yu.

"Xiao Yu, your eyes have not deceived you. This withered leaf did indeed rip my sleeve."

Lifting his head toward Sword Peak, he answered, "If I'm right, then this leaf has been imbued with dangerous chi from the mountain peak! I can already deduce that the Hero Sword won't be the only incredible thing we see… There is a feeling of a peerless sword chi! A chi that seems to say it can kill anything, be them men or gods; it is a crazed, arrogant sword chi!"

Hiro's assumption was of course correct!

On top of Sword Peak, there was a crazed, arrogant sword chi -- crazed and arrogant because it belonged to the saint of swords!

Sword Saint!

The now forty-two year old Sword Saint had been standing by the two Hero Swords since he failed to draw them out!

It was because he could not admit defeat!

He would not!

He would not because he had already reached the status of a saint. With his grand stature, these two Hero Swords refused him even after he made this long and arduous journey. He could not come within two yards of the swords. They would rather shatter than be drawn by him!

Those damnable Hero Swords!

Sword Saint was ruthless; he would never abide by someone else's rules! He brought his Peerless Sword to the top of the mountain, clearly because he disregarded the rules that he felt applied only to the ordinary swordsman.

But since being humiliated by the Hero Swords, he was greatly angered, yet he still had not destroyed them!

He did not destroy the Hero Swords because he respected them too much, as all swordsmen do. He did not covet them, or the Nameless Sword Technique written upon them. Though the Nameless Sword Technique could allow one to know all sword techniques, Sword Saint firmly believed that he was already beyond that level!

He had allowed these two swords to continue existing, because he wished to completely subjugate them!

He still remembered when he was five how much he loved learning about the sword. He was so enamored that he even gave up the one true love of his life: Lan, the woman he loved more than anything in the world. Yet in the end he left her as well!

All for his obsession with the sword!

The sword had never disappointed him. All swords have submitted to the Sword Saint!

Only these two Hero Swords had not, and would rather shatter than submit!

It was hard for Sword Saint to accept, for he had been a sword master all his life. With his noble personage, how could these two ugly swords reject him? Is he not the one who could pull out these swords -- the legendary Heaven Sword?

No! Sword Saint would not believe it! He could not believe that although he had reached saint level, there was another higher level that surpassed him -- that of the Heaven Sword!

These past decades, since Sword Saint had begun to study the sword, he climbed Sword Peak countless times, attempting to draw the Hero Sword, but failed each time. After each failure, he practiced more diligently. He felt that he had not reached the level needed to draw the Swords. This was the eighth time he had made the attempt on Sword Peak…

And it was the most grievous disappointment he ever encountered in his life!

He had already deciphered the Holy Spirit Sword Skill Twenty-One. He felt confident enough that within the next ten years, he would be able to create Sword Skill Twenty-Two. He had already reached his current limit, so if he failed in pulling out the Hero Sword now, he would have to go back and practice again!

It would be another ten years of practice!

So this was the last time, the last time that Sword Saint would make the attempt! He stayed by the Swords' side. He didn't want to leave so quickly in defeat!

Try as he might, no matter how hard, the Hero Swords would not yield to him. They stood silently as if rebuking him for trying too hard. Why? Why? Why?

Just then in the dead silence of Sword Peak issued the sound of a water drop...

It was the sound of a teardrop falling on the snow.

Ah! It's…

He's shed a tear?

The Hero Swords seemed to be watching his tear!

The world seemed to be watching his tear!

Even the gods above watched this rare tear drop!

Because he is a peerless warrior, he should never shed any tears!

But who can understand Sword Saint's heart? Who can understand his tear?

Only Sword Saint himself knew! He stared hard at his teardrop and spat out two words.

"Hero! Sword! Since I picked up the sword at age five, I have never shed a single tear! Even when Lan left me, I wasn't the least bit sad! But now the two of you have made me angry enough to shed a tear!"

Sword Saint's chest rose and fell rapidly. With his chi, he should always be calm and collected; it is easy to see how much this upset him!

Even more frightening, the teardrop on the ground had started to steam and eventually evaporated from his heated glare! His eyes fell upon the two Hero Swords; it was a malicious glance, filled with the intent to kill, and he finally called out.

"Fine! Hero Swords, since you are so high and mighty that you would rather perish than submit to me, I won't let anyone else have you either!"

His eyes narrowed and he continued, "I don't want to see you, or be humiliated by you again! The best way is to destroy you!"

Sword Saint's anger boiled over, and he could no longer contain himself. He suddenly lifted up his Peerless Sword and slashed out towards the Hero Swords! He was going to destroy them!

Just as his sword came within two inches of the Hero Swords, the two swords began humming! As if they were crying!

Sword Saint laughed maniacally.

"Haha! Hero Swords, you're finally scared of me? Are you willing to submit to me now? You finally know that I am the peerless champion? Hahahaha…"

With his crazed laughter, Sword Saint continued his verbal attack; he was determined to destroy the Hero Swords!

At the last moment! Sword Saint stopped!

He stopped because a strange feeling gripped his heart!

He felt two terrible forces converging upon Sword Peak! Yes! He's sure that he is right! These two forces made even the Sword Saint wary with fear!

At the same time, the two Hero Swords began humming again!

Sword Saint was shocked.

"What? So you weren't begging me for mercy? You are calling for your masters? What? Those two forces I feel approaching, are they the masters you have been waiting for all these ages?"

"But these two forces, one of them feels unstable. Why? It's like he does not wish to possess this awesome strength! Hehe, very good! I want to see who these masters are that the Hero Swords have been awaiting for

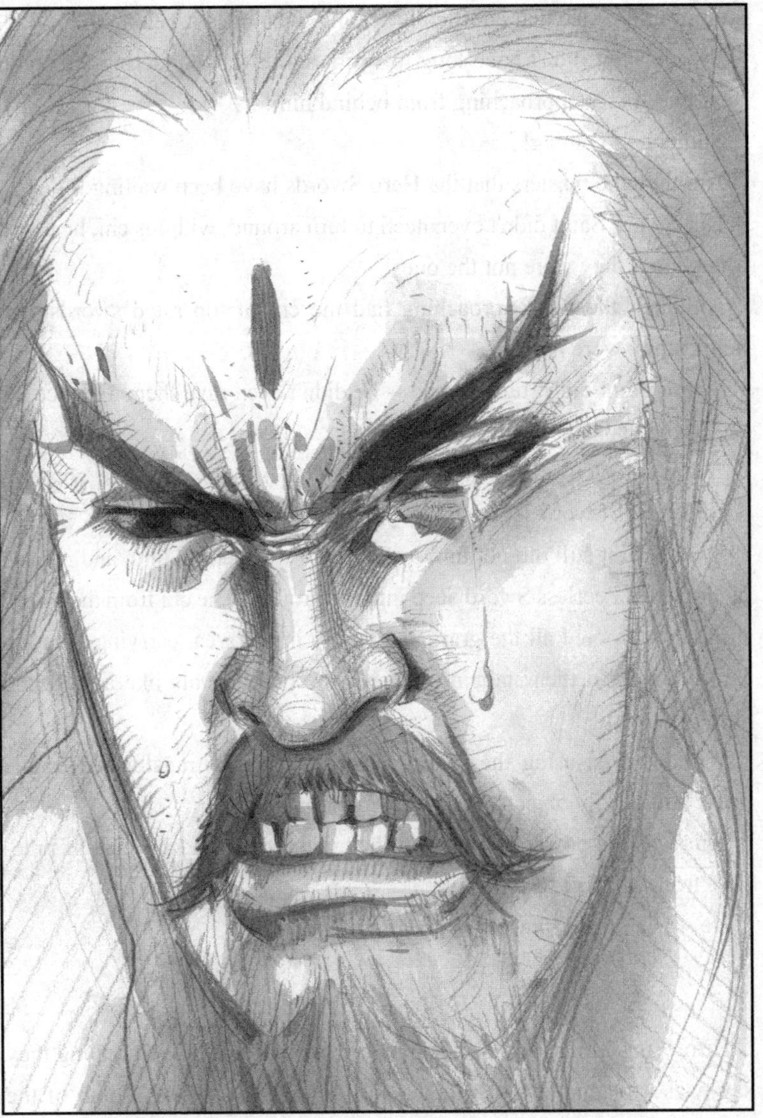

so faithfully. Also that conflicting feeling, who does it belong to?"

Sword Saint didn't have long to wait! As he was pondering, he could hear two forces approaching from behind him!

Someone's coming!

Are they the masters that the Hero Swords have been waiting for?

No! Sword Saint didn't even need to turn around, with his chi, he could already tell they were not the ones!

Although the two approaching had the chi of top rated swordsmen, heroes they were not!

Sword Saint didn't turn around -- he didn't even give them a glance, as he laughed coldly.

"Although you are good swordsmen, you should not have come to Sword Peak! I won't let trash like you waste my time! Leave!"

Sword Saint still did not turn to face who was behind him, and instead he drove his Peerless Sword deep into the ground! The chi from the sword instantly uprooted all the grass and leaves in the area, carrying them up into the air and then stabbing towards the two arrivals like a thousand sharp swords!

Without even using the sword, Sword Saint had transformed fragile grass into deadly objects. What incredible power!

This was the power Sword Saint had gathered from his years of practice, from age five to forty-two.

He was a sword himself -- a peerless sword!


Hiro, Ying Ming and Xiao Yu neared Sword Peak. The first thing they saw was a plaque at the entrance carved with the words "Tomb of the

Great Sword Master". The numerous swordsmen that have come have erected this memorial to the Great Sword Master!

The second thing they saw was a stream of blood!

It was the blood of the two brothers, Sword Dragon and Sword Tiger!

Alas! When Hiro, Ying Ming and Xiao Yu looked closer, they saw that a thousand blades of grass had completely pierced through the brothers' bodies. They looked like two bloody porcupines stuck full of quills!

Such powerful martial artists! For Sword Dragon and Sword Tiger to die so quickly, was incredible. They only had time to cover their chest with their gold and silver swords, but it was not enough. Their entire body was pierced full of grass blades. Even the swords in their hands were shatter by the flying grass. Though they were still alive, they had been wounded grievously.

Who had such incredible powers? Who could defeat these two top ranked swordsmen -- in a matter of seconds -- to within an inch of their very lives? Who could be so cruel and cold hearted with their power?

It's him!

Hiro, Ying Ming and Xiao Yu all collectively looked upon the strong figure standing next to the Hero Swords! They no longer had time to admire the Hero Swords. The man standing by the famed swords had not even turned around to see who he had injured. With his deep yet compelling, powerful voice, he spoke, "Trash! From the sound of your stance as you blocked my blades of grass, I can already tell one of you used a sword carved with a dragon and the other, a sword carved with a tiger. You must be the newly famous Dragon Tiger Twin Sword brothers?"

Without even turning his head, Sword Saint was able to deduce the shape of their swords from the sound alone! His years of obsession with the sword were clearly shown.

"Hehe! I don't care if your swords are carved with a dragon or tiger, or even if they are worth thousands of gold taels. Let me teach you something here, you see, the sword is not for *looking*, it is for *fighting*! Using swords as a symbol of your worth will only bring about your own destruction!"

Sword Dragon and Sword Tiger lay prone upon the ground, and while still conscious, they could say nothing. Their throats had been pierced with the blades of grass as well. If they were to speak, blood would gush from their wounds. In shame, they held their tongue.

Still with his back turned to the group, Sword Saint's ears twitched slightly. It seemed he had felt something, and continued speaking. "The ones I have been waiting for are here! All right! Let me see the mighty heroes that the Hero Swords have been waiting for? What manner of creatures are you?"

With that, Sword Saint abruptly turned around and stared directly at Hiro and Ying Ming!

Hiro stared almost rudely back at Sword Saint! Only Ying Ming's eyes stayed dull!

"It is you?" Sword Saint's eyes focused on Hiro alone!

Sword Tiger and Sword Dragon stared evilly at Hiro, but Hiro was unfazed. He was never afraid, and perhaps that was his greatest fault -- it pushed him to the brink of death. Coolly he questioned back, "Do you know me?"

Sword Saint laughed coldly, "Of course I know you, although I have never met you, but when you were in your mother's womb, you already had the chi of a sword ruler. How could I not remember so special an

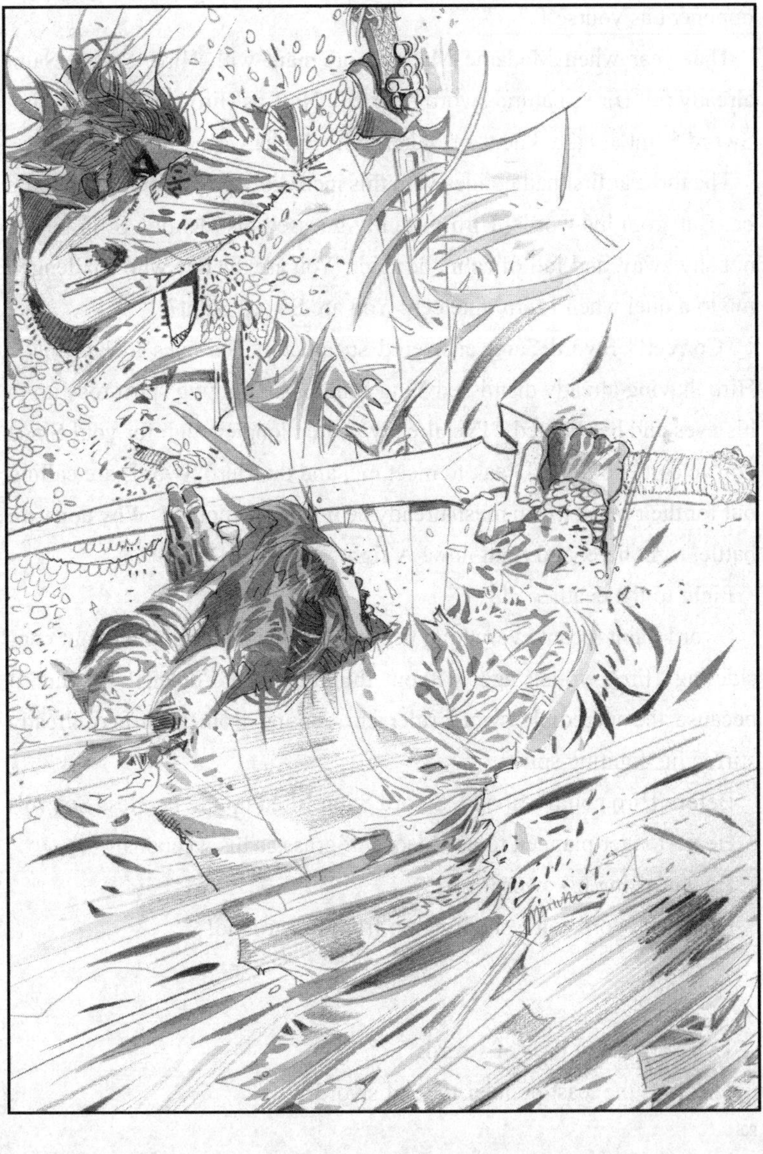

opponent as yourself?"

That year when Madame Mu was pregnant with Hiro, Sword Saint already felt Hiro's natural sword ruler chi. Now as Hiro stood before him, Sword Saint already knew, or rather, felt who he was!

The three at first had no idea who this incredibly powerful master could be. But from his words, Hiro instantly guessed his identity. Still, he did not shy away, and full of calm, he said, "You are the one who challenged me to a duel when I turn nineteen! You are Sword Saint?"

"Correct!" Sword Saint answered succinctly! His eyes locked in on Hiro, having already dismissed Ying Ming. The fighting spirit rose up in his eyes and he shouted, "I've already waited long enough for you! Since you've come to Sword Peak to meet me, and the Hero Swords are calling out for their master, you must already be powerful enough! Why don't we battle, right here, and right now! A fight! To! The! Death!"

Fight to the death?

Sword Saint meant everything he said! They would fight, without considering Hiro's young age, without thinking of the details! He did so because the incredible sword ruler chi coming from Hiro had already stirred his fighting spirit!

Before Hiro could respond, Sword Saint lifted up the Peerless Sword!

He no longer planned to use blades of grass as his weapons!

He was using his sword!

Peerless Sword came shooting up from the ground!


There are many type of swords!

The 'it' is the least popular type of sword!

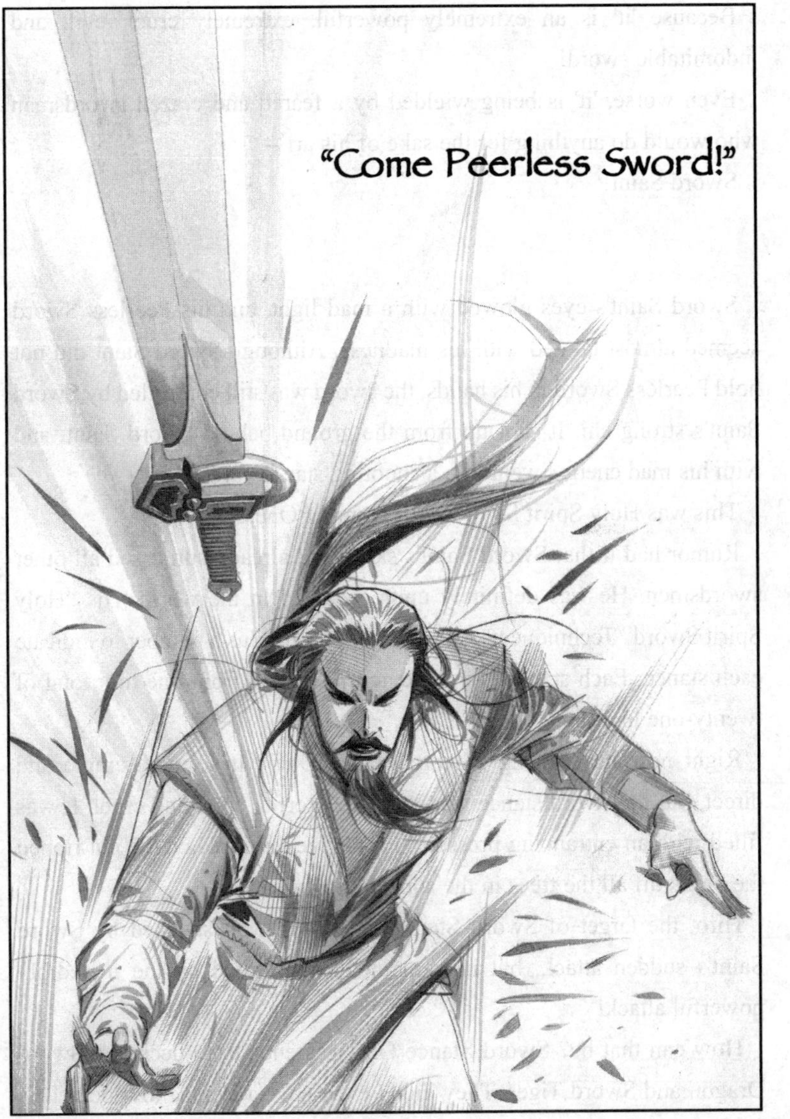
"Come Peerless Sword!"

Because 'it' is an extremely powerful, extremely cruel, evil, and indomitable sword!

Even worse, 'it' is being wielded by a feared and crazed swordsman who would do anything for the sake of his art --

Sword Saint!

Sword Saint's eyes glowed with a mad light, and his Peerless Sword seemed almost tainted with his madness. Although Sword Saint did not hold Peerless Sword in his hands, the sword was still controlled by Sword Saint's strong chi. It shot up from the ground behind Sword Saint, and with his mad energy, went like a shooting star towards Hiro!

This was Holy Spirit Sword Skill Number One!

Rumor had it that Sword Saint's skills had already surpassed all other swordsmen. He was definitely unprecedented in the world. His "Holy Spirit Sword" Technique uses the word "sword" plus a number to indicate each stance. Each stance is unique and powerful, from one to a total of twenty-one in all!

Right now he is using "Sword Stance One". It seemed simple and direct, but the sword stance was quick, powerful, sure, and cruel. It was filled with an entrancing pressure. From five yards away, the chi ripped the barks off all the trees in the surrounding area.

Hiro, the target of Sword Stance One, was a bit shocked by Sword Saint's sudden attack, but he remained unperturbed by the incredibly powerful attack!

How can that be? Sword Stance One was enough to decimate Sword Dragon and Sword Tiger. They didn't even have a chance to block. This

# The Battle That Should Not Be

was Sword Saint's oldest attack, so how could Hiro hope to withstand it? Sword Dragon and Sword Tiger were certain that it would be impossible for Hiro to escape. Perhaps because he was so egotistical, or maybe just ignorant, Hiro didn't seem to understand Sword Saint's power!

Xiao Yu was frightened by Sword Stance One's power, and exclaimed, "Brother Hiro! Run!"

Hiro heeded not Xiao Yu's warning, his mouth turning up in a confident smile, the smile he often wore. In fact, Sword Saint's sword was faster than lightning; he could not run away even if he tried.

How could Hiro just smile? Sword Dragon, Sword Tiger and Xiao Yu could not understand. Only Ying Ming, the one forgotten by Sword Saint, understood the reason why. But he stayed expressionless, his eyes glistening with a hint of admiration for Hiro!

Why did he admire Hiro?

Was it because he could already tell what Hiro was going to do?

He admired Hiro's courage!

Hiro did not try to dodge Sword Stance One. He thought of an ingenious way to defeat the attack!

Just when Peerless Sword closed to within mere inches of Hiro, he suddenly lifted his bare throat towards the sword!

What was he doing!

Was he seeking death?!

Sword Tiger and Sword Dragon could not believe their eyes; they thought Hiro must have been driven mad with fright! Xiao Yu screamed!

Only Ying Ming stood silent, but his eyes were cheering for Hiro!

Just when everyone thought Hiro's death was certain, suddenly Peerless Sword stopped in front of him!

Although Peerless Sword had stopped, Sword Stance One's power continued unabated towards the giant tree standing behind Hiro. Instantly, the mighty tree was splintered and destroyed!

What a frightening Sword Stance One! If Sword Saint had not stopped, Hiro's head would surely have separated from his body already. But why did saintly fighter cease his attack?

Sword Saint's face showed great anger; he glared at Hiro.

"How dare you! No one has ever looked down upon my Saint Sword Techniques so! No one dared to face it head on, though they know it is impossible to avoid!"

Sword Saint continued to focus his energy on Hiro, he did not look once at Ying Ming. Perhaps because Sword Saint felt Ying Ming had no fighting spirit! Sword Saint did not consider him a worthy opponent!

Hiro laughed wickedly, "Really? It is because people did not dare face you head on? -- that is why they died all the quicker. Since you are a saint and so maniacal, you must love it when they try to evade. Otherwise, if they really were able to dodge, where would that leave you?"

Hiro insulted Sword Saint, calling him a maniac and crazed. Xiao Yu, Sword Tiger and Dragon could not believe it, but Sword Saint did not become angry. Perhaps because he always thought the best of himself, he just stared back at Hiro and answered coldly,

"So that is why you didn't even try to dodge my sword?"

Hiro confidently answered, "Of course! I've studied all types of Sword Styles these past five years, but my favorite is still my father's Palm Techniques. If you insist on competing using the sword, then I admit I am not as good. You are also breaking your promise to wait until I turn nineteen; you are clearly in the wrong. Since I know I cannot avoid it, why bother, I will break your stance, my way!"

Upon hearing the word break, Sword Saint's face froze! His tone became suddenly icy.

"Hehe! Punk, do you know what you are saying? Within the past twenty years, no one has ever broken a single stance I used. I haven't even heard the word 'break' in over two decades. You're saying that you were trying to break my stance?"

Hiro remained calm as ever.

"That is so! You've been practicing the sword for how long now? You don't even know the basics of the sword? There are no limitations to the sword. It does not always take a sword to break a sword stance, there are always ways -- as long as you can break the stance! It seemed as if I was risking my life, but that's how I broke your stance! See? You weren't able to kill me, right?"

Hiro boldly called his seemingly reckless actions a calculated maneuver. Sword Saint was angered beyond belief, but with years of training behind him, he maintained his composure for the time being. Gritting his teeth, Sword Saint retorted.

"Pah! You have a clever mouth! You think I won't dare kill you? I was just curious why you were so eager to kill yourself."

Hiro smiled again.

"Ha! Sword Saint! That's why I am smarter than you! I knew that you would be curious enough to stop your attack! I was trying to lure out your curiosity -- that was my strategy! Don't forget when two swordsmen duel, aside from strength, skill, and philosophy, they are also competing in strategy! Just based on this first stance, you have already been defeated by me in terms of strategy!"

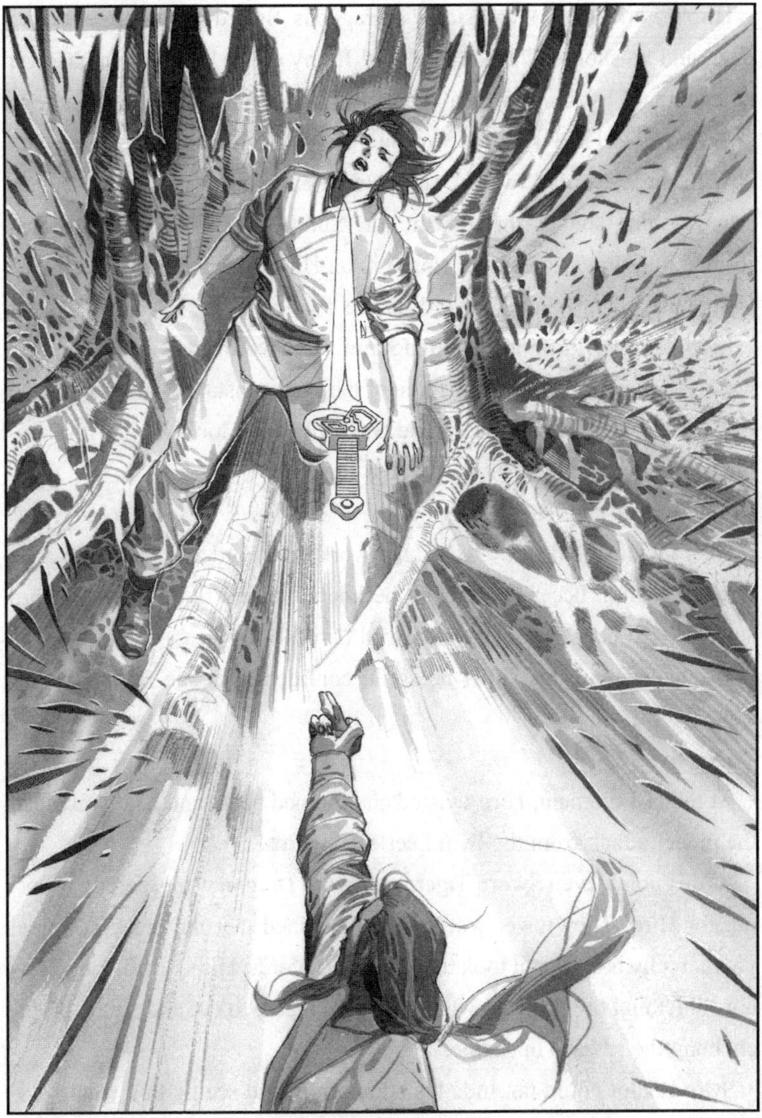

Hiro's words grew increasingly outrageous. Sword Saint's anger boiled over, and he shouted, "How dare you! In my entire life, no one has ever defeated me! Even my master eventually lost to me and died beneath my sword! We will see what other techniques you know besides strategy!"

With these words, Sword Saint's Peerless Sword ascended and made two swishing sounds through the air! Suddenly Peerless Sword transformed into two swords, and closed in on Hiro from the front and back.

This was Sword Saint's Sword Stance Two!

Instantly transforming the strength of one sword into two, the stance was even more powerful. The force of the stance instantly snapped all the trees in the area. Sword Tiger and Sword Dragon looked on with complete awe, and Xiao Yu even forgot to scream.

But Hiro just smiled slightly!

His previous bold tactic would not work on Sword Saint again! Yet he remained calm, because although he knew that his five years of sword studies were no where close to Sword Saint's forty years of practice, he still felt that with his skills he could confidently dodge Sword Saint's stance!

Exactly!

At the last moment, Hiro twisted and jumped back, and neatly avoided the pincer attack from the twin Peerless Swords!

At this point, even Sword Tiger and Sword Dragon were secretly cheering for Hiro. They never would have imagined that the brash, arrogant youth, really had what it took to back up his words. His skillful dodge was not something the brothers would have been able to do, and so the brothers hung their heads in shame.

Sword Saint could not hide his admiration, and seeing this young sixteen year old boy with the same skills that he once had at sixteen, he could not help but praise Hiro.

"Very good! If you don't die today, then one day you will be a worthy opponent for me! But now you will never have a chance!"

As Hiro flipped back away from the Peerless Swords, the two swords collided in midair with a loud boom! One of the swords instantly disappeared, as it was only an illusion created by Sword Saint's incredible chi. The real Peerless Sword suddenly made a sharp turn and shot back towards Hiro! It flew like it had eyes, bearing down on Hiro!

This was the real Sword Stance Two!

This attack had multiple levels! There was a second level of attacks!

The turn of events surprised Hiro greatly, but he quickly reacted! Eying the Hero Swords embedded not far from his side, he had an idea!

Shifting his position, he flew in front of the Hero Swords and yelled.

"Sword Saint! I am standing in front of the Hero Swords. If your stance were to really kill me and pierce through my body, you would shatter the Hero Swords as well. Don't you want to draw the Hero Swords?

Very smart! Under the present circumstances, he had no weapon and no way to avoid the attack, by using the Hero Swords as a shield and counting on the fact that Sword Saint could not bear to destroy the Swords, Hiro made a gamble. But Sword Saint merely laughed cruelly.

"You guessed wrong! You think I would not destroy the Hero Swords? No, before you even arrived here, I already planned to destroy the Swords! Now is the perfect opportunity to get rid of you and the swords!"

This came as a great shock to Hiro. He could not imagine one so obsessed with the sword would now simply destroy the Hero Swords! It is too late for regrets, he has no time left!

The Peerless Swords were less than two feet from Hiro, too close to dodge. The only route left was to try and block the attack head on!

But with no weapons in hand, how would he defend against the Peerless Sword?

With his life hanging by a thread, Hiro suddenly had another idea, and maybe his last idea: If he could just draw the Hero Sword.

He could use the legendary Hero Sword to block Peerless Sword!

With that thought, Hiro quickly stepped back. This was what Sword Saint wanted to know anyway, if someone like Hiro, with the sword chi of a ruler, could be the master the Hero Swords had been waiting for. Was he good enough to be called a hero?

Hiro stepped back, and reached for one of the Hero Swords. Was he the master? Indeed no one has ever come within two yards of the Hero Swords. If anyone were to step within a closer distance, then the swords would shudder as a warning, and ultimately shatter in defiance!

Hiro's step had brought him within that two yard radius. His whole body was filled with tension, not knowing if he could avoid Sword Stance Two, and not knowing if he was the Hero Sword's master.

He heard it! The sound of a loud crack…

Just as the legends recalled, the sword showed signs of defiance. Did this mean Hiro was not its rightful master?

He was not the one that the Swords had been waiting for? It was not him? He was not the one?

In that short instant, Hiro felt a twinge of disappointment. It was not that he really coveted the Hero Sword, but the feeling of rejection weighed down on him.

But Hiro judged too quickly! Because…

Only one of the Hero Swords cracked! The other remained perfectly intact and seemed to beckon him!

One Sword rejected, while the other did not. Did this mean that he was the master of one of the swords?

But then who was the master of the other Hero Sword?

At such a perilous moment, there was no time for Hiro to ponder any further. He did not even have time to draw the Hero Sword! Because the Hero Sword that accepted him was the one further away, and the Peerless Swords were only a foot away!

He had no time left!

Peerless Sword was only half a foot away from Hiro's face. With no weapons, Hiro did not quietly wait to accept death.

"Sword Saint!" he loudly screamed. "You and your sword are too cruel! Do you think just because you wish someone dead that they must die? I don't believe that you can kill me!"

He then put all his strength and chi into his palms -- the Mu Family Palm Technique; he was planning to catch the blade with his bare hands!

He's giving it all he's got!

No one had ever survived an attack by the Peerless Sword! No one would dare to use his bare hands to stop Peerless Sword!

If there was such a person, then he must be a mad man! A courageous man! A man as crazed as Sword Saint!

Even Sword Saint was surprised to find this young man was as mad as he. The young man was using his bare hands to catch the blade?

Under the force of Hiro's palms, a change occurred.

Hiro caught the Peerless Sword!

Though Hiro trapped the blade between his palms with his impressive display of power, it was not enough to ward off Sword Saint!

At the last moment, the Peerless Sword struck out multiple times towards Hiro's head. Now the tip of the blade was mere inches from Hiro's face!

Sword Tiger and Sword Dragon thought Hiro dead for sure. Xiao Yu's tears fell down with worry. Sword Saint was enjoying the battle and surprised at Hiro's courage, but still no one had survived before, and he did not want to break his record!

Today, he would kill Hiro!

Those that he wanted dead could not escape!

Yes, Hiro would certainly die, if no one stood up and helped him right now...

But there was someone that no one thought had the strength to help!

In that life and death moment, Hiro saw a figure dashing for his back and he heard two loud sounds! A pair of steady hands came from behind him and swept by his face. As Hiro had done, his two palms reached for the Peerless Sword, hoping to catch it.

With an earth shattering boom, under the duress of "four" palms, the tremendous powers of the Peerless Sword was completely halted!

Everyone on the cliff was stunned!

Sword Dragon and Sword Tiger were awestruck! They would never have imagined that the person who stepped in with bare hands to help Hiro would be "him"! It was that person they thought was just following Hiro around like a dog!

Xiao Yu was stunned! She never though he could or would dare to save Hiro from Sword Saint's mad attacks!

Sword Saint was stunned! He was stunned because the one who saved

Hiro was someone he completely overlooked. That person seemed to have no fighting spirit within him, and Sword Saint did not feel that he was worthy of consideration! But who knew, that when he helped Hiro, he would become a completely different person! Fighting spirit beamed from his eyes, like a sword, a heavenly sword!

Heaven Sword!

The one who stepped in and helped Hiro catch the Peerless Sword's blade was the one who had been numbly standing by!

Since Madame Mu died five years ago, he was forced to fight once again for Hiro!

Finally because of Hiro, he stepped into this battle that should not have been a battle!

Hiro could not believe that Ying Ming -- who had been wasting himself away, not wishing to advance his martial arts, whose powers should be far beneath his own -- had the power to help stop Peerless Sword. That must mean that Ying Ming's potential was limitless! While Hiro was thinking these thoughts, an incredible thing happened!

On top of the now silent Sword Peak, two cries could be heard!

Everyone looked towards the origin of the sound! It came from the two Hero Swords!

They were calling for the masters who were so near!

The Hero Swords called.

After Ying Ming ran to Hiro's back and helped him stop Peerless Sword, he had stepped into the forbidden zone of the Hero Swords. Yet strangely, the two swords showed no signs of rejection!

Did that mean, like Hiro, Ying Ming was one of the Hero Sword's long awaited masters?

There could be no doubt! With the two cries, the Hero Swords showed everyone the answer!

Their masters were here.

Suddenly the two swords flew up into the sky of their own accord! As they reached a height far above the peak, the outer stone shell encasing each sword suddenly exploded!

With the outer shell shed, the true form of the Hero Sword was revealed after millennia. Their outward appearance was plain and unadorned, much like other swords of their time. Yet the light coming from the Hero Swords was chillingly bright, outshining Peerless Sword!

Ah! After centuries of patient waiting, at last the true features of the Hero Swords were revealed!

Synchronized, the two Hero Swords fell downward and embedded themselves respectively in front of Hiro and Ying Ming, like two faithful servants awaiting their masters' command!

The swords had not forsaken the intentions of their creator, the Great Sword Master. They waited through the long years, willing to shatter rather than submit, and finally they had found their rightful masters!

Everyone's face showed the same incredulous look! Even Hiro and Ying Ming could not have imagined that they were the rightful masters of the Hero Swords!

Sword Tiger and Sword Dragon were even more alarmed. They had just made fun of Ying Ming, only now to discover that he was in fact a master of the Hero Sword -- a real hero!

Xiao Yu was jubilant! She knew that Ying Ming would eventually fulfill the hopes of his birth mother and Madame Mu, to become a real hero. Now the Hero Swords had found Ying Ming and Hiro?

Sword Saint stood in awe and disbelief!

He could not believe what he had just seen! He could not believe that those the Hero Sword had been waiting for were two sixteen year old boys! It was not him!

Even a saint of swords was not enough?

"Impossible! Impossible! Impossible! Impossible..." Sword Saint pointed at the two Hero Swords, losing all composure.

"Hero Swords! You were waiting for these two? Are you blind?" he yelled. "How dare you not submit to me? You would rather submit to these two worthless children?"

His hatred burned. His humiliation peaked. Sword Saint could not control his anger, and he damned the heavens.

"Are you mocking me? Are you mocking me? Do you know what I have sacrificed for the sake of the sword? I have sacrificed my own life! My dignity! My beloved! Now you are telling me, I am not the most powerful, legendary Heavenly Sword? Gods! Are you mocking me?"

Losing any semblance of control, Sword Saint pulled back the Peerless Sword and began hacking at the heavens!

In an instant, Sword Saint had slashed more than three-hundred times across the skies. Suddenly, the force of his attacks blocked out all light as if the very heavens were hiding from his wrath!

But Sword Saint was not satisfied, and continued slashing towards the heavens, getting angrier, more bitter, and crazed with each slash until his attacks became too fast for the human eye to follow!

He slashed towards the heavens thousands upon thousands of times. Finally a lightning bolt streaked down from the darkening clouds. Peerless Sword was once again stabbed into the ground in front of Sword

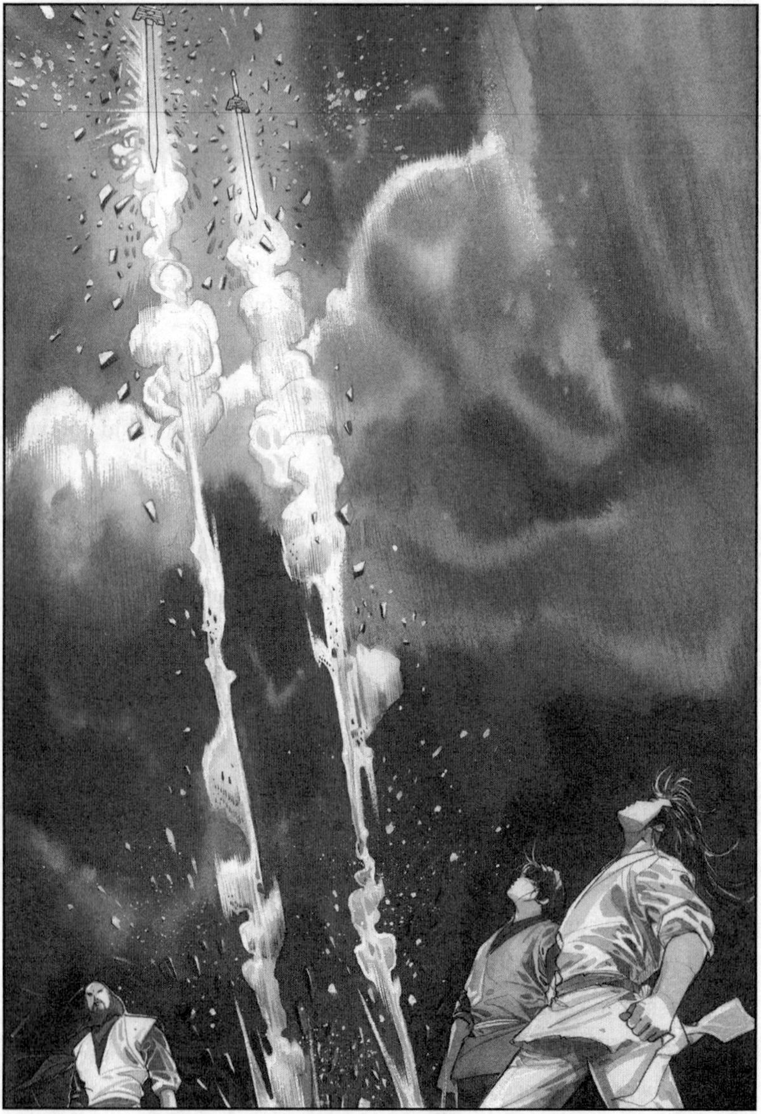

Saint, and the ground around was completely shattered!

He finally stopped!

Sword Saint had his back towards everyone, panting heavily. Like an immortal that had been cast down from the heavens, proud yet utterly alone.

He muttered to himself, "Impossible! Impossible! How can the gods anoint these two as sword legends, yet I remain only a saint! Impossible! I won't allow it!'

Seeing the heartbroken Sword Saint, Hiro and Ying Ming could not help but feel sorry for him. This middle-aged man had sacrificed everything and still had been rejected by the Hero Swords. Hiro and Ying Ming looked at one another, both feeling pity for Sword Saint.

But it was too early to pity the Saint! Sword Saint's voice turned evil!

Extremely evil!

"Impossible? Haha! I am already a god, a saint; there is nothing that is impossible! Since the heavens have decreed one of them will be the legendary Heaven Sword, then I will change the impossible to possible, I will…"

Sword Saint turned back, eyes filled with envy, and glared at Hiro and Ying Ming.

"Punks! Since the two Hero Swords accepted you as their masters, then that means one day, after the trial of the two swords and one is broken, the person remaining with the intact sword, will be the swordsman named by the Great Sword Master: the Heaven Sword. If I want to change the impossibility of me being the Heaven Sword to the possible, then the fastest way seems to be killing the two of you!"

Yes! Sword Saint's words rang true! If he wanted to change the truth of what cannot be, then he must destroy those that can achieve what he can not! Although Sword Saint may never become a heaven sword, he could still be the highest ranked swordsman in the land!

Hiro and Ying Ming could not have predicted this turn of events. For Sword Saint had turned down a darker path. Even worse, Sword Saint's sword was angrier! Crazier! Quicker!

It exploded!

Drawn out by Sword Saint's incredible chi, Peerless Sword once again pulled from the ground. Filled with madness he screamed, "I have nothing against you, but today, you must die! You can celebrate together in hell!"

With lightning speed, Peerless Sword once again divided into two swords and shot towards Hiro and Ying Ming respectively! "Sword Stance Three!" Sword Saint called.

Why was this stance called "Three"? Since it was three, should there be three swords? Why was it just like Sword Stance Two? Hiro and Ying Ming did not have time to think about the details, because Sword Three came even faster and with more power, at least twice that of Sword Two. Hiro and Ying Ming quickly leapt back to dodge the attack, but Peerless Sword followed closely behind.

Even odder, as the two of them dodged to avoid the attack, Hiro continued to dodge from Sword Three, but Ying Ming stopped. Strangely, the sword chasing him stopped before him and vanished into thin air!

Ying Ming's actions greatly shocked everyone. The ones most in awe were the two figures hiding in the corner: Sword Wisdom and Sunder.

"Ah! What incredible sword wisdom!" Sunder stared at the place where the sword disappeared. "Father, you should not look down on the black-clothed youth! His chi is far below that of the one dressed in white! But his understanding of the sword is greater. It seems as if he just chose a random place to stop, but that position was exactly the weakness of Sword Stance Three. That was how he seemed to diffuse the attack without seemingly trying!"

Sword Wisdom nodded in agreement.

"Perhaps I've underestimated him! At least, I never would have guessed that one of the Hero Sword's masters would be him..."

Sunder spoke up again.

"Father, the death of their fate as Heaven Swords, is secondary! Since the Hero Swords are now freed, are we going forward with our plan?"

"Yes!" Sword Wisdom answered. "The Nameless Sword Technique is written on the tips of the Hero Swords. It is imperative that we steal the Hero Swords from them before they see it. We cannot allow two people outside of our 'Sword Clan' to be stronger!"

So Sword Wisdom and Sunder are descendants of the Sword Clan created by the Great Sword Master?

Yes, since the Great Sword Master created the Sword Clan many years ago, many sword schools sprung up, but none were as powerful as the Sword Clan! The Sword Clan had become almost lost within the flow of time, becoming increasingly mysterious. Many people heard of its name, but no one knew its location!

Sword Clan was the strongest of all sword schools! But their leader, Sword Wisdom feared the day that the Sword Clan might not be the strongest!

The Great Sword Master created the Nameless Sword Techniques and said that only those fated to be the Heaven Sword could understand it. It was useless to those who were not fated. Though the Great Sword Master carved the Techniques on the Hero Swords, he also passed it down to the leader of the Sword Clan!

But sadly, though the Nameless Technique had been passed down through each generation and each leader had completely memorized it, none had ever been able to understand it. That is why Sword Wisdom and Sunder must steal the Hero Swords to prevent the ones who draw them from understanding the Technique. If those thieves were to learn the Nameless Technique before the Sword Clan, how could the Sword Clan remain the strongest?

So they must prevent the masters of the Hero Swords from obtaining the Nameless Sword Techniques!

Just as Sword Wisdom and Sunder were debating when to steal the Hero Swords, Ying Ming had easily dodged the Peerless Sword mirage chasing him. Meanwhile, the Peerless Sword chasing after Hiro seemed to be the real one. After several close encounters, Hiro was worn out and desperate.

Sword Saint saw how easily Ying Ming found the flaw in Sword Stance Three, and his anger multiplied. But he could not help but praise Ying Ming.

"You are very wise in the way of the sword! The position you seem to have chosen at random is the fatal flaw of Sword Stance Three! Although it seems that you have no fighting spirit, let me tell you that aside from myself, you are the best of all the swordsmen here on this peak!"

Aside from Hiro and the Sword Dragon, Sword Tiger brothers, it also included the hidden Sword Wisdom and Sunder. With Sword Saint's superior skills, it seemed that he was already aware of their spying; he just felt it unnecessary for them to know of his awareness.

Ying Ming remained emotionless even with Sword Saint's praise! But Hiro was the one who felt proud for his brother.

"Of course, old man! You better be careful! If my brother doesn't die here today, then he will surly defeat you one day! Haha…"

Hiro should not have said that, for this pushed Sword Saint back into his dangerous anger.

"The impudence!" he shouted. "I will kill you all the quicker for that!"

Quicker? How will he make Hiro die quicker?

With those words, Sword Saint flew into the sky. His body seemed to turn into a giant Peerless Sword stabbing madly for Hiro!

This is the true Sword Stance Three!

Sword Saint himself was the last of the three swords!

He was the true Sword Three!

Gods!

Peerless dashed through the sky! Sword Saint's fingers struck out like lightning! No matter how confident and intelligent Hiro was, he would never have time to respond. Ying Ming saw Hiro falling in an increasingly desperate situation! Even the normally calm Ying Ming shouted, "BROTHER!"

Xiao Yu screamed, "Hiro!"

Ying Ming dashed with the fastest possible speed he had ever used in this lifetime, desperate to reach Hiro!

He had to stop Sword Saint from killing Hiro! He can't allow the tragedy that happened with Madame to occur again!

He already owed her so much!

At the same time Ying Ming was rushing towards Hiro, from a darkened corner of Sword Peak a voice shouted out, "They are busy killing one another! Now's our chance! Sunder, my son! Take the Hero Swords!"

A strong figure ran like a sprinting elk from under the darkened cover towards the Hero Swords. It was Sword Clan Sword Wisdom's son Sunder, laughing haughtily.

"Haha! While the bird and fish fight, the fisherman captures both! The Hero Swords are ours!"

Or so Sunder thought, as his hands were about to close around the hilts. Yet at the last minute, a strong yet soft chi lifted the Hero Swords straight into the air. Sunder was momentarily stunned.

"What? This soft chi... it is very similar to the 'Karma Reincarnation' used by the famed 'Monk King'. Is that meddlesome old bag here?"

As Sunder pondered, a white-robed figure fluttered down, and with a sigh he spoke, "Although my Master asked me to merely observe and not interfere in their destiny, I cannot allow the Hero Swords to fall into the wrong hands. How can I just stand by doing nothing?"

Sunder looked closely to see a young monk robed in white, around his own age with a patient and kind face. Another sigh followed as the young monk spoke once again, "Dust to dust, ashes to ashes! The Hero Swords belong to the two of them, and should return to those two brothers. Hero Swords, return to your rightful masters... Go!"

With these words, Bushi lifted his hands and using the chi from his palms, gently grasped the Hero Swords from midair and tossed them respectively towards Hiro and Ying Ming.

Bushi, a name that is synonymous with truth, had promised his master he would not interfere, but he could not just watch the despicable actions of Sword Wisdom and his son Sunder.

Using Karma Reincarnation, he passed the Hero Swords to Hiro and Ying Ming so that they could use the swords to fight Sword Saint.

In fair combat!

Hiro and Ying Ming didn't know that there were so many people on Sword Peak. But they knew that the young monk was trying to help them. Quick as lightning, they each grasped one of the swords!

In the instant their hands touched the Hero Swords, they both felt deep within the swords a soul that immediately linked to their own. It was as if they were trying to tell them a long-kept secret.

"Is it the Nameless Sword Technique?"

Yes! The Nameless Sword Technique seemed to be seeping into their minds!

But it did nothing to help the situation! Although Bushi wanted them to have a fair fight, it was still too late!

Until they could fully comprehend the Nameless Sword Technique, Sword Saint's sword was still the quickest in the world!

Faster than Bushi ever thought possible and faster than Ying Ming and Hiro could block with the Hero Swords!

Faster than lightning! Sword Saint's Peerless Sword aimed straight for Hiro's face, and Sword Saint's fingers stabbed towards Hiro's pressure point! He wanted to break Hiro's martial art's ability before killing him.

[*Editor's note: In Chinese martial arts, it is possible for a highly trained martial artist to destroy another's ability to circulate chi by destroying their chi meridians through vital pressure points. Sword Saint is aiming for a spot on Hiro's lower stomach, known as the tandien. This is the focal point of a person's chi.*] He wants Hiro -- his most hated -- to die a horrible death!

"Haha! I will destroy your martial arts ability at the same time I kill you! Even when you die, you will die a useless pile of trash!"

Sword Saint laughed maniacally, his fingers continued stabbing towards Hiro. Hiro tried his best to block the attack, but he knew, though his Hero Sword might knock away the Peerless Sword, he was powerless to stop Sword Saint's fingers from stabbing into him!

No! He can be saved!

Because there was one person, no matter how horribly Hiro treated him, who would willingly die for Hiro! He would rather become that useless pile of trash in his stead!

Just as Sword Saint's fingers were about to stab into Hiro, Ying Ming shouted desperately.

"BROTHER!"

Ying Ming's eyes became full and his voice full of passion, "I will take your place!"

Take his place? Take Hiro's place?

Ying Ming didn't have time to use his Hero Sword, using his fastest possible speed, he turned his body into a fearsome Heaven Sword and stepped in front of Hiro...

Sword Saint's fingers stabbed through Ying Ming's tandien and painfully disrupted his body's chi. Ying Ming's martial arts ability was destroyed at that moment! Sword Saint's fingers were like a sharpened blade, piercing Ying Ming's stomach and emerging out his back, through his pressure point. This stab, as Sword Saint predicted, not only would have turned Hiro into a pile of useless trash, but would also kill him!

Even Sword Saint could not have predicted Ying Ming's heroic attempt to save Hiro! Everyone was stunned!

A stream of hot blood sprayed over Hiro's face dripping down his forehead and chin. He could not have known, the Ying Ming he constantly tormented would still risk his life for him. All his regret flooded to the surface, and he shouted to the bloodied Ying Ming.

"BROTHER!"

Xiao Yu's tears came streaming forth. "Brother Ying Ming!"

Hiro would never call Ying Ming trash again! His real feelings finally poured forth, and he called him brother -- a brother that he respected!

Ying Ming heard Hiro call him brother, even though blood was gushing from his wounds. And although death beckoned, he smiled.

He said, "Big... brother, you called me... your brother?"

Ying Ming, with his dying breath only cared about that simple courtesy, and Hiro's eyes grew misty.

"Don't say anymore! Ying Ming. No! You are the hero that my mother admired and you were always... the brother that I most... admired!"

Ying Ming smiled, blood gushing from his wound and trickling from his mouth.

"Really?"

"Big brother, actually I've always known that you were just... being mean to me... on purpose. It was mother's dying wish to ask... you to spur me on, right?"

Facing his dying brother, Hiro's could not stay cold-hearted any longer and finally nodded in agreement.

"Yes! Everything I did was because of Mother's last wish! She asked that no matter what, I would have to help you get back your will. She hoped that you wouldn't disappoint your birth mother's hopes of becoming a real... hero!"

Ying Ming smiled bitterly.

"But I was always kind of useless," Ying Ming said. "I have forsaken your mother and my mother's hopes. I've also forsaken... everything that you have done. Now not only are my martial arts skills gone, but I am... dead..."

"No!" Hiro cried. "Brother, you have always done so well! You are braver than anyone! Even braver than I! You are a brother that I am proud of! You are the real *hero*!"

"Really?" Ying Ming smiled bitterly once again. His voice was getting weaker, but he continued speaking.

"I... am so happy, because today... I can hear you call me... brother. That feeling is just like that year when mother called me her... Ying Ming. It's that... loving life... is so wonderful... after all. It's just that simple; just to hear my big brother calling me... brother... that... simple..."

With that, Ying Ming's bloody body slowly sank to the ground; his breathing began to slow. Hiro held him close, as he felt Ying Ming's life flowing out.

"BROTHER!" Hiro screamed! Madly! Despairingly!

No! He can't let Ying Ming die like this! He carries the hopes of his mother Madame Mu and his birth Mother Autumn, also the hopes of the Great Sword Master as a heavenly sword who is a hero of the land. He can't die like this! Hiro would rather trade his own life for Ying Ming's!

But he felt Ying Ming's body grow gradually colder, his breathing get-

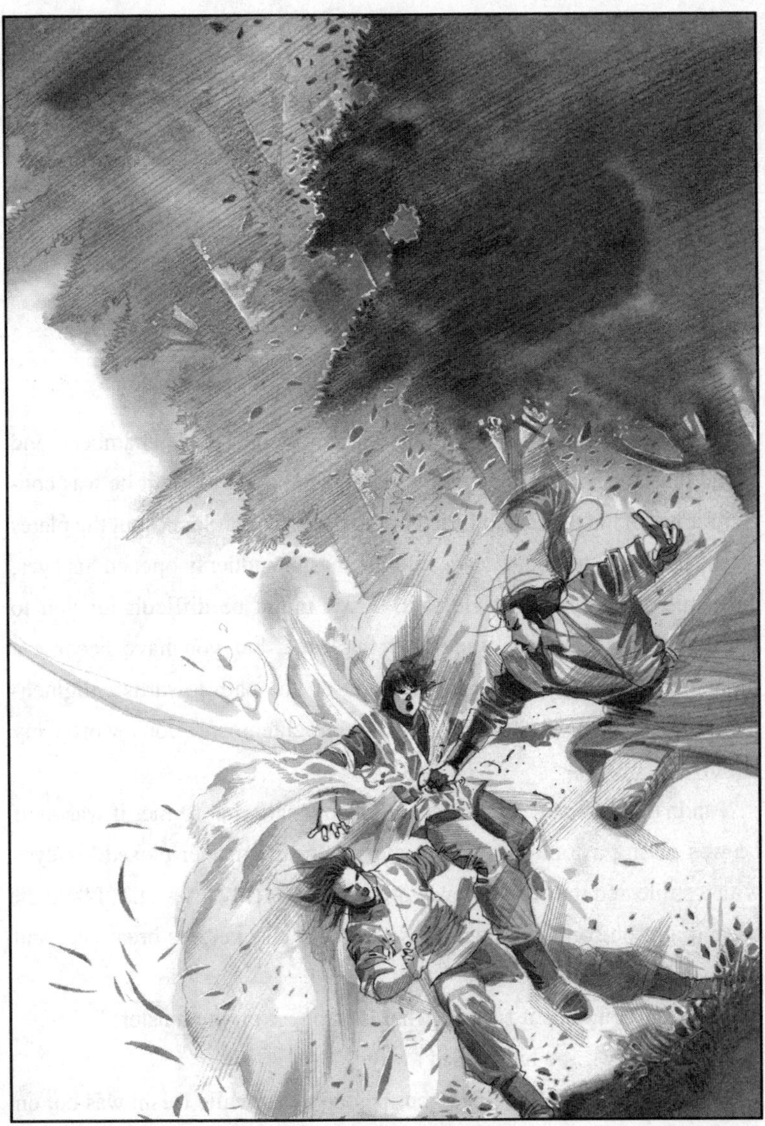

ting slower. Now that he no longer even had the chi to protect himself, he who had yet to become a hero, was closer to death -- he would die young, and there was nothing that Hiro could do!

Just when Hiro felt lost in sorrow, a pair of hands touched him on the shoulder!

It was a pair of very, very calm hands.


"Oh no! Oh no!"

"What's the matter?"

"I… I just brought some food to Master Monk King's chambers, and found that… he was praying with his eyes closed. I thought he was concentrating on his prayer, so I tried not to disturb him. So… I put the plates on the table and turned to leave, but the master suddenly opened his eyes, and smiled kindly at me. He said, 'Fa, it might be difficult for you to understand the ways of Buddha at this time, but you have become a monk, and that means you are stepping on the path towards enlightenment already. One day you will reach enlightenment, don't worry, my child!

"I didn't understand why master suddenly said that to me, it was as if he was giving a fond farewell to me! Then, the master closed his eyes with a smile and muttered a few words, and suddenly grew still. I thought there might be something wrong, so I boldly checked his breathing, and found that, on my..."

"Fa, can't you keep it simple, what is wrong with the master?"

"Master… he… he has passed away!"

"What? Master Monk King… has passed away while Bushi was out on assignment? What did the master say in the end? Who did he wish to take over as head master?"

"No, no, no! It was nothing like that! I don't really understand what he meant, but master said,

'Life in reverse, justice is rare;

Love is a flame, then men dive in as the fire phoenix;

If a phoenix does not die, how can it be reborn?

If a hero does not die, how will he know real love?

Bushi, Bushi, do you still not…

Understand?'"

A sword can be loved.

A sword can also return love.

That was Ying Ming's final thoughts before death.

Just as his eyes sagged to a close, his heart beat slowed, and grew weak. He faintly sensed the Hero Sword falling to the ground, enveloped in a misty light.

The light of a teardrop.

It's as if this Hero Sword, linked to Ying Ming, was crying for the fate of the master it had waited thousands of years for. The tears of a sword.

If a sword could feel love, then a human being should feel even greater love.

Ying Ming felt Hiro's hands on him, and they felt especially heavy. It was as if he didn't want to let go of his useless younger brother. Hiro's admiration for Ying Ming finally burst forth like a flood that had been unleashed!

He didn't want him to die! Not only because of his mother's dying wish, but also because he truly admired him!

In the moment of his death, Ying Ming faintly saw Xiao Yu's tearful face. She cared for him, he always knew that.

Even the powerful Sword Saint seemed touched by Ying Ming's death. The hand on Hiro's shoulder remained steady. A steadiness that seemed to say he already foresaw Ying Ming's death, and that everything was as destined. Who was this person?

There was someone who watched everything calmly: Bushi!

The white-robed Bushi!

Just as Ying Ming could no longer see Hiro, his heart finally began to stop, and he knew he was really going to die!

Thump - thump!

Thump - - thump!

Thump - - - thump!

Thump - - - - thump!

The sound of his heart stopped...

He could hear nothing at all.


There is a really old fairy tale.

The fairy tale states that what the phoenix people see is a bird that will never die.

Every five hundred years, it dives into a fire, only to be reborn from the ashes.

The phoenix that is reborn is completely transformed, more dazzling than before, and more beautiful!

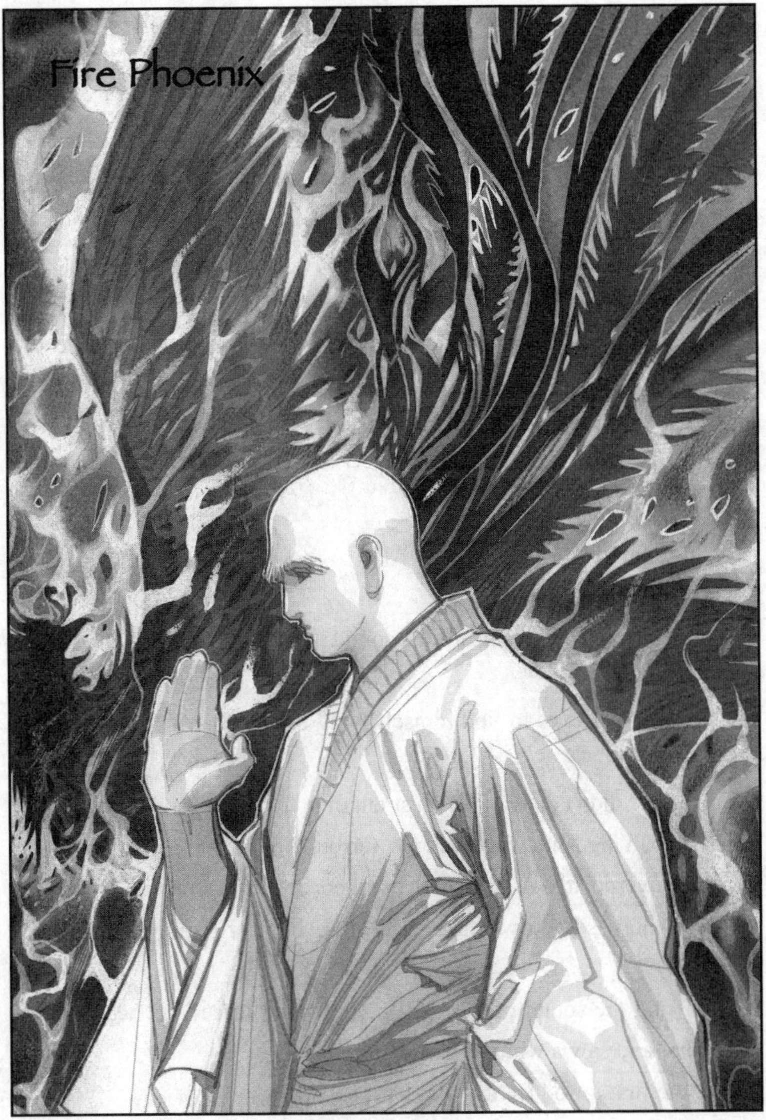
Fire Phoenix

But the cruel flames, and sea of fire, are a difficult thing to endure.

To be reborn, one must suffer the heat, and let one's body die within the sea of flames, and float away as ashes!

It is like a warrior that cuts off his own arm to save himself!

If the eternal fire phoenix was a human being instead of a bird...

If that person died for love and honor, can he be reborn?


After countless moments...

Thump - - - -

Thump - - - thump!

Thump - - thump!

Thump - thump!

Thump thump!

Thump thump!

Ying Ming once again heard the sound of a heart beating -- the beat of his own heart!

He opened his eyes to find himself lying on the altar in an old temple. He was alive!

Though he didn't die, he had no strength in his body. Struggling to push himself up, Ying Ming surveyed his surroundings.

"Don't overdo it!" A calm voice called out from outside the temple walls. "Otherwise you will use up all the chi your big brother put into your body!"

Following the sound of the voice, Ying Ming turned his head toward the doors, and saw a white-robed monk!

"Let me first introduce myself! I am called Bushi!"

"Bushi?" Ying Ming was slightly surprised, the monk seemed about seventeen years old. He looked to be very young, probably not very learned in the ways of the Buddha, yet he had a calm face that seemed untouched by any calamity. Either he was well along the path to enlightenment, or he was extremely powerful in the martial arts.

Perhaps this monk was both.

"That's right! I am named after the Truth from the Holy Scriptures." Bushi said with a slight smile. "Luckily I was there, otherwise you... ah, thinking back, my master, the Monk King, asked me to observe your fate in hopes that I might come to understand some greater truth, and perhaps he already knew that you would suffer such a fate, and would need my assistance..."

"So you are the one who brought me back from the brink of death?"

Facing Ying Ming, Bushi did not try to boast.

"Actually you were only half saved by me. My master, the Monk King, is not only a clairvoyant, but also well learned in the ways of philosophy and medicine. My martial arts and medical skills are directly learned from him. Even if Sword Saint pierced through your body, as long as you had one breath left in you, I could still save you, but... You were first broken of your martial arts skills by Sword Saint, and then impaled. It was an extremely dangerous wound, and not something simple medical procedures could heal. To live, a skilled martial artist needed to permanently sacrifice his internal chi to protect your heart meridian, or else you would have died. That was the only one way to save you!"

"How?"

"Using my Karma Reincarnation and the chi sacrificed by another martial artist, one strand of chi was turned into full life energy and then placed in your body. With this, your heart could be protected so that you would not die from internal injury."

"But," Ying Ming seemed to have awakened fully, "It would be difficult for any martial artist to build up his chi. I am just a useless person, who would sacrifice their hard-earned chi for someone like me?"

"You don't really need to ask that question. I believe you already know the answer," Bushi replied kindly. It was obvious he was proud of the one who sacrificed their vital chi to protect Ying Ming's life. His character was honorable, enough so to make someone proud.

True! Bushi's words struck home! It was no longer necessary to ask. Ying Ming already knew who willingly sacrificed his chi for him…

"Is it… my big brother?"

Bushi smiled without speaking and after a moment, he said, "Moments before you were about to die, that young man who was trying to steal the Hero Swords -- I believe his name was Sunder -- was trying to prevent you and your brother from becoming one with the swords and thus obtain the Nameless Sword Technique. But he was too late. Using my Karma Reincarnation I was able to pass the swords to the two of you. When you grasped the Hero Swords, he gave up, because you had already obtained the Nameless Sword Technique, it was useless for him to steal it."

Yes, Ying Ming understood that! When he touched the Hero Sword, he already felt a strange sense of connection with the sword. It was as if the Nameless Sword Technique was imprinted in his mind, in fact…

He still recalled it!

He also understood it, completely!

Bushi said, "That young man Sunder was hiding with his father Sword Wisdom. They belong to the powerful Sword Clan. Seeing their plan fail,

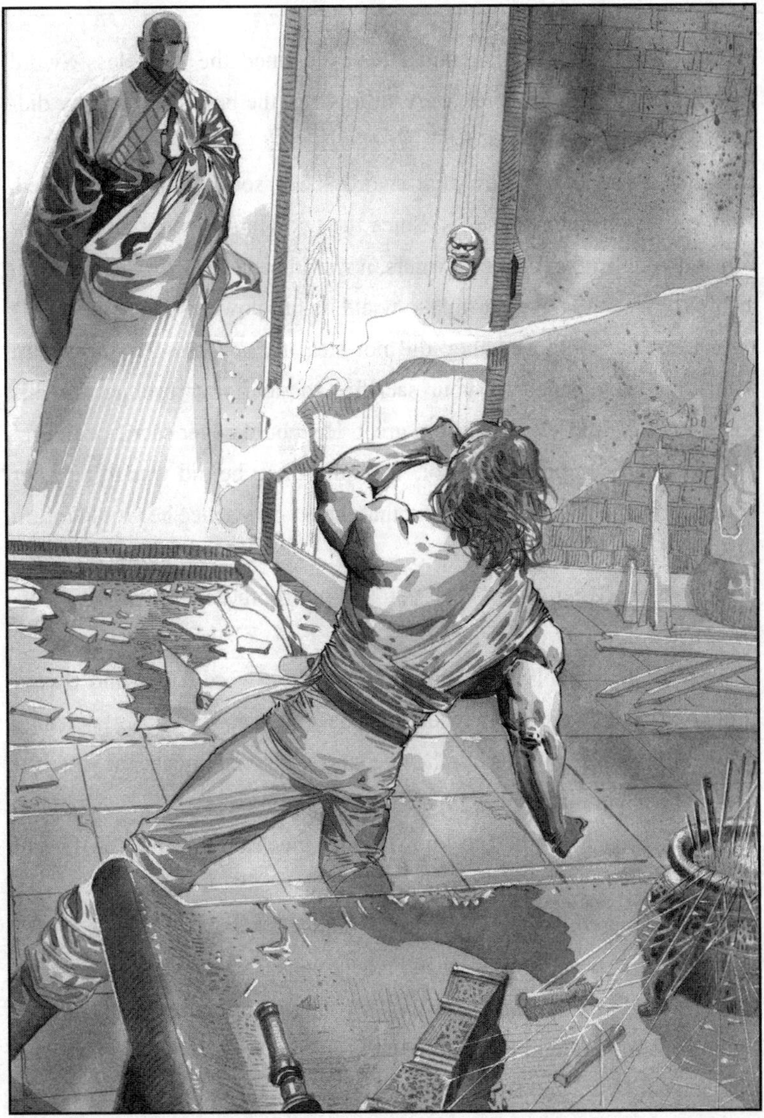

the father and son left."

"But, though my brother and I have obtained the Nameless Sword Technique, the Hero Swords were still two of the best swords; why didn't they take the swords away?"

"Most swordsmen know that swords have souls," Bushi answered, "and know who their owner is. Since the two Hero Swords already saw you and your brother as their owners, it would be useless for them to steal them. They would never be able to wield its full power, so they gave up!"

"You are lucky indeed they did not steal the swords. As for Sword Saint, he was touched by your sacrifice to save your brother. Yet his obsession with the sword was too great. He would never sacrifice his chi to save you, or remedy his error. The only thing he did was to let your brother go temporarily. But he said that three years hence he would return to fight again as promised!"

Sadly, Ying Ming said, "Then you and my brother were the only martial artists left on Sword Peak?"

Bushi sighed deeply once more, "Yes. The Sword Tiger and Sword Dragon brothers were badly wounded. I needed to use my skills to change chi into life force, so I was not the one who sacrificed my chi for you. But your brother voluntarily gave his chi to save your life…"

"Then," Ying Ming had to know, "How much chi did he sacrifice to save me?"

Bushi answered calmly, "Perhaps I shouldn't have told you. You see, your brother was very upset when he held you. He was madly screaming at heaven and earth for taking away his younger brother. He said the high hopes your mother and his mother had for you were all wasted! He said that he would save you, even if he had to give up the entire chi in his body to do so. You are also a martial artist; you know if a martial artist were to instantly give up the entire chi in his body, he would be near death as well. Luckily I was there, I stopped him from passing his entire chi to you, so that he could still have 5% left to sustain himself…"

5% of his chi? Hiro only has 5% of his chi left? That means he used 95% of his chi to save Ying Ming?

Ying Ming drew a deep breath, he had always known that Hiro's berating was his way of trying to spur Ying Ming towards greater things, but he would never have imagined that Hiro was really so kind to him!

Ying Ming lifted his head and sighed, "95%… of his power? Big Brother, you… sacrifice too much for me."

Bushi shook his head, "Too much or too little is never a set amount. In your eyes, it may be too much, but in his eyes, it may not have been enough to express his feelings for you! You would've died for him, and he would've sacrificed all his power and died for you. How much or how little is no longer important! The most important thing is that…"

Bushi came out and told Ying Ming this most important lesson; he felt that Ying Ming already understood. The most important thing was that both of them were still alive, and they could live from now on as brothers should.

Ying Ming suddenly thought of something else, and asked, "Then how is it that only you and I are here? Where is my brother and… Xiao Yu?"

"Don't worry! We found this abandoned old temple to give you time to recover! We've spent a whole night here saving you! Now that the worst of it is over, your brother and Xiao Yu have gone to look for food and prepare a carriage to take you home."

"Take me home? I am better already. I can walk home on my own right.

Why do I need a carriage to take me home?"

Hearing this, even Bushi was moved, and seriously he told Ying Ming, "Don't forget, Sword Saint pierced through the most vital pressure point on your body, and destroyed your martial arts ability! You are only an ordinary person now!"

Ying Ming was stunned; no wonder he felt so weak upon waking! This was not only from his injuries, but also because he has lost all of his martial arts ability.

Bushi continued, "Your brother and I used all of our strength and barely saved you from the brink of death! As for the martial arts ability you lost, there is nothing further I can do! Also, you have been wounded deeply by Sword Saint--even if you were to recover, you will be much weaker than an ordinary person. Just walking two or three miles a day would completely exhaust you."

Only a few miles a day? Weaker than an ordinary person? Then does that mean he is not even as good as a normal person? He is a... useless person? Ying Ming's face changed as he heard the news.

Bushi's eyes shone, he tried asking Ying Ming a question.

"So what do you think? Do you regret your decision to risk everything to save your brother?"

"No!" Although Ying Ming seemed shocked, he quickly recovered and answered without hesitation.

"I would never regret it! Even if it were to happen again, I would do the same thing! Also, I never cared for getting more martial arts ability. It doesn't matter if I lost my chi! I've always wanted to be an ordinary person anyways..."

"But..." Bushi seemed to want to say something more, but just then, a calm voice spoke from outside the door.

"Bushi, don't say any more. What's wrong with being an ordinary person? Perhaps it would turn my brother's bad Lone Star fate around, wouldn't that be a great thing?"

The voice was clear and loud, it was easy to tell who the speaker was. Hiro!

Hiro and Xiao Yu had come back with a horse-drawn carriage.

They walked slowly into the temple. Seeing Ying Ming awake, Xiao Yu was ecstatic, she forgot herself and ran to embrace Ying Ming's hand.

"Brother Ying Ming, you're finally awake? You're fine now!"

She suddenly calmed herself, and while holding Ying Ming's hands, her face turned bright red and she quickly let go. But her eyes showed signs of happy tears; it was easy to see her joy at his awakening.

But Ying Ming looked only at Hiro. Hiro was happy that Ying Ming was feeling better. Ying Ming didn't know what to say to his brother, and stammering he said, "Big brother, I..."

He was grateful for all that Hiro had sacrificed to save him, but Hiro seemed to be smarter than he thought possible, and before he could say it, Hiro already chimed in.

"Brother, you don't need to say that. What you're thinking is also what I am thinking. Since we both know what the other is thinking, there is no need for words. No matter what is said or not said, from now on..."

With that Hiro placed his hands on Ying Ming's shoulders and said with absolute conviction, "We will always be the... best of brothers!"

From now on, they would always be the best of brothers! Though Hiro was not always kind to Ying Ming, that had all been put behind them now. One was willing to die for the other, while the other willingly sacrificed

95% of his power to save his brother. There was no need for words of thanks between the two. Isn't it better that these words remained unspoken in their hearts?

Ying Ming understood what Hiro was trying to say, he nodded his head and put his hand over Hiro's hand, "Yes, no matter what is said or not said, we will always be the best of brothers!"

Hiro laughed happily and Bushi and Xiao Yu joined in as well.

And so it came time to bid Bushi farewell.

Hiro, Ying Ming and Xiao Yu thanked Bushi for his help in saving Ying Ming. They had already been gone from the Castle for a whole day and night, it was time to head back.

Since Ying Ming was not fully healed, Hiro was afraid that he might be further hurt from the journey back, so he personally placed Ying Ming inside the carriage with Xiao Yu to care for him. There was one more seat to the right, and Hiro turned and glanced at Bushi standing near, asking, "Bushi, thank you for everything! Do you need a ride?"

Bushi shook his head, and said mysteriously, "Thank you for the kind offer! But I still have business to attend to; I won't be able to come with you."

Hearing that, Ying Ming and Xiao Yu stuck their heads out and Ying Ming asked, "Bushi… will we see you again?"

Bushi looked to Ying Ming and cryptically said, "Don't worry! We will meet again! Don't forget what I said before -- my master, Monk King asked me to observe and learn something from your destiny. To fulfill that, I must definitely see you again!"

"Promise?" Hiro also chimed in; it seemed that he also wanted to see Bushi again, because this little monk was different from all the other annoying monks he'd met, who only knew how to chant litanies.

"Promise!" Bushi answered.

What important thing did Bushi have to do that prevented him from traveling with Hiro and the group?

After seeing the three of them off, Bushi turned slowly and walked once more inside the temple.

Entering the temple, he sat down slowly cross-legged and began circulating the chi within his body. After several moments, he coughed out a great clot of blood. The stain spread through his pure white cassocks.

"What a mad… cruel… Sword Saint!" Bushi wiped away the blood at the corner of his mouth and continued to circulate his chi. Sword Saint's last stance was more than enough to kill Ying Ming, even if Hiro gave up his entire chi.

But seeing the two brother's struggle, and knowing that Hiro's chi would not be enough to save Ying Ming, Bushi had to do something. He did not want these two bothers' fate to end thus, so while he used Karma Reincarnation to pass on Hiro's chi, he also gave 50% of his own chi to Ying Ming, hoping that it would be enough to save him.

Using so much of his own chi while wielding Karma Reincarnation, strained and injured his system. He did not want Hiro or Ying Ming to know the severity of his injury, lest they feel bound to repay his kindness. He pretended to be fine, but the moment the three left, he had to heal himself.

After three days of chi circulation, he finally recovered. The bleeding stopped and his injuries were finally under control.

"Sword Saint, why must you be so cruel to a sixteen year old boy? You destroyed his martial arts ability, but now if he doesn't die, he will find a way to get those abilities back. Then his martial arts ability and sword skills will be far greater than yours! He will be the best in the entire world! Why do you rush to destroy your best opponent?"

What? There is a way for Ying Ming to get his martial arts ability back? Is this something his master Monk King had foretold?

Bushi continued circulating his chi and healing his injuries. His half closed eyes fell to the ground and focused on something!

There were several broken bricks lying on the floor of the temple, and some seemed to have words carved on them. The carvings were not very deep, so the person carving them must not have used or possessed any chi. But even without chi the carving was still there, and they read, "Bushi, I was unconscious for a long time, but when I awoke, I knew that the chi that saved me was not just my older brother's. There was another strong chi mixed in, and I knew it had to have been you!

You and my brother have sacrificed so much to save a worthless person like me; I don't know what to say. But I just want to say one thing: thank you. Friend."

Friend?

This last word sent warmth rushing into Bushi's heart.

These words must have been carved by Ying Ming while Hiro, Bushi and Xiao Yu were gone. He knew Bushi did not want them to know how much he had personally sacrificed to save him, so he wrote these words to silently thank him.

Friend.

The word was all too unfamiliar to Bushi. When he drank the Tea of

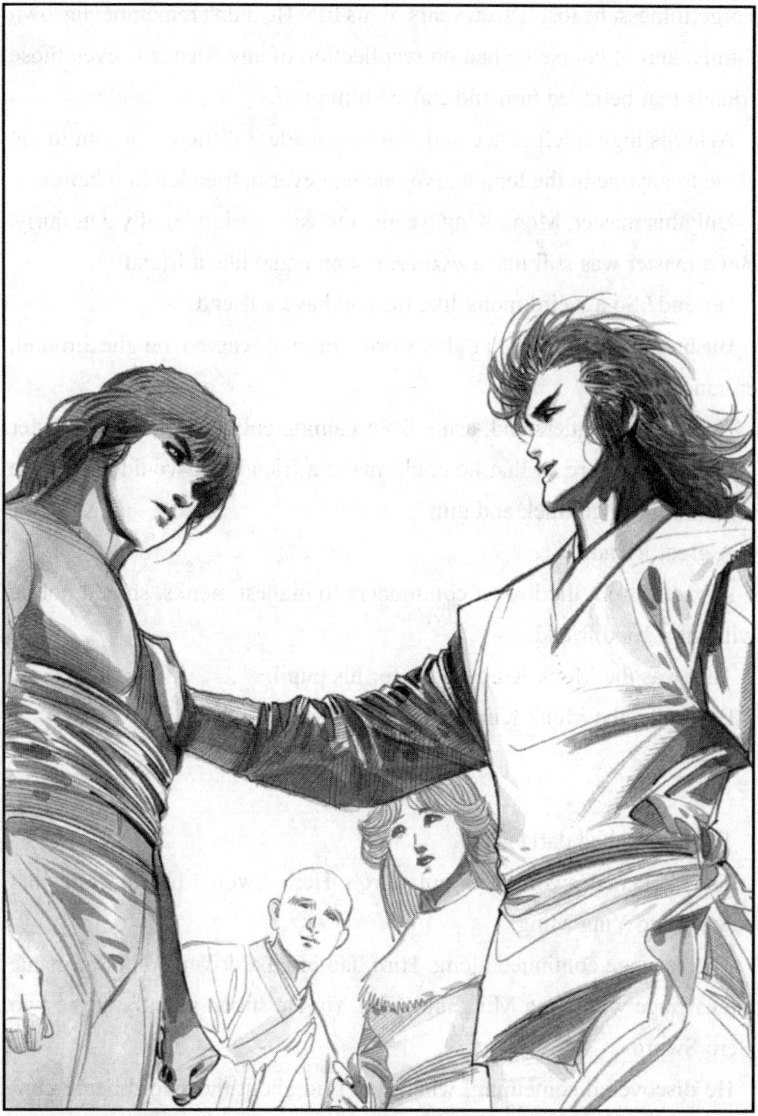

Forgetfulness, he lost fifteen years of his life. He didn't remember his own family, and of course he had no recollection of any friends -- even those friends that betrayed him and caused him grief.

Also his high intelligence and odd past made it difficult for him to get close to anyone in the temple. No one had ever befriended him before.

Only his master, Monk King, seemed to care for him kindly and fairly. But a master was still just a *master*, not an equal like a friend!

"Friend? So a weird monk like me can have a friend?"

Bushi looked intently at the word "Friend" carved on the ground, entranced.

He began to understand, aside from gaining enlightenment, his master also sent him here so that he could make a friend that would always be with him through thick and thin.

A great friend!

All men, from the lowest commoners to highest monks, should not be without a good friend...

That was the Monk King's wish for his pupil.

But sadly, the Monk King had passed away.


The Sword had darkened.

The darkened sword was not Hiro's Hero Sword, but the one that belonged to Ying Ming!

The carriage continued along. Hiro had hired a driver, so he sat inside the carriage with Ying Ming and Xiao Yu. He stared intently at the two Hero Swords.

He discovered something, what they said about the sword being connected to its wielder was absolutely true!

The two Hero Swords, one shone brightly, while the other remained dull, representing the fate of it's respective master…

One master had sacrificed 95% of his chi, but with diligent practice that chi would return. Plus knowing the Nameless Sword Techniques, his future would only grow brighter!

The other had his martial arts skill destroyed. Although he had understood the Nameless Sword Technique, there was nothing he could do with it. He was as weak as a child; his fate must be as dark as his Hero Sword!

But was there truly nothing that could be done?

Hiro tried to think of something, anything that would help restore Ying Ming's powers!

The already sleeping Ying Ming suddenly woke up, and through half closed eyes, he said, "Big brother, I know what you're thinking about."

Hiro tried to brush it aside.

"Oh? Have you learned to see through my heart as well? How do you know everything I'm thinking of?"

Ying Ming looked at him and said, "I know you must be thinking if there is any way to get my internal powers back."

When he spoke, Xiao Yu was awoken, and she promptly asked, "Brother Hiro, it's already happened, don't think too hard on it. Even if you try, there is nothing you can do."

Hiro smiled bitterly, not admitting defeat, "I know, I've been thinking non stop for a way to restore your powers. I think it is so unfair! How could someone like you end up as an ordinary person? People like Sword Wisdom, Sunder, even Sword Saint, who are obsessed with the sword, why are they so strong? Why is the world so unfair?"

Ying Ming barely had the strength to smile.

"Perhaps," Ying Ming began, "that is fate! I can not run from fate, even if I tried."

"No!" Hiro insisted, "I don't believe in fate! I don't believe that nothing can change fate! I believe you control your own destiny!"

Seeing Hiro so emotional, Ying Ming put his hand on Hiro's shoulder and tried to persuade him.

"Big Brother, I know you are just doing your best for me, but like Xiao Yu said, it can't be helped. If you continue worrying, you will only get sick! Besides, like I told Bushi, what's wrong with just being an ordinary person? This is my true wish! Really, I just want to live normally. I know even my birth mother would have wanted me to live happily, it might be a lucky thing to live a normal life."

Really? Is that what Ying Ming really wished?

Hiro turned and looked squarely at Ying Ming, and after a long moment of silence, he finally sighed.

"I understand. If you just want to live a normal life, then I understand. But I promise you, I will take care of you from now on! I won't go back on the promise I made to mother!"

Living a peaceful ordinary life is a type of blessing…

Also, having the word of someone honorable like Hiro, to take care of everything -- what more could one ask for?

But there was also something that could happen.

What if Hiro were to die one day before Ying Ming?

What if one day, Hiro was not around…

No matter what, Hiro had made a promise to look after Ying Ming, and he would do as he promised. Just as his mother, Madame Mu had desired, so he would endeavor to see it come to pass.

One day later, the three finally returned to Castle Mu…

It was twilight when they reached the opulent Castle.

Mu Long was usually busy, yet he waited anxiously outside with the door servants. Seeing Hiro return, he smiled happily, the worry gone from his face; he cared greatly for his son.

But seeing Ying Ming inside the carriage, with a bandage around his stomach, he cruelly said, "Ha! Hiro and Xiao Yu have been gone for more than a day; I was worried and asked people to search everywhere. But it seems that they were fine all along, but because you got hurt, they had to delay coming home!"

For so many years, Mu Long continued to treat Ying Ming cruelly. Even now when Ying Ming was hurt, he still had to endure Mu Long's taunts.

Hearing his father's scolding, Hiro could not help but to defend Ying Ming.

"Father! Please don't say that! Ying Ming didn't hold back Xiao Yu and me! Just the opposite, it is I who caused him to suffer so! I… caused his martial arts ability to be destroyed!"

Even Mu Long was shocked to hear this news. But he didn't care too much for Ying Ming, so he did not ask how this came to be. A cruel smile appeared on his face.

"Hehe! So what if this trash lost his ability? Hehe! He deserves it! He killed your mother! I'm happy he's gotten what he deserves!"

He glared once again at Ying Ming, and Ying Ming lowered his head.

Xiao Yu could not just stand by, even if Mu Long was her uncle, she spoke up.

"Uncle, actually auntie's death… was not all Ying Ming's fault. It's not really fair to blame everything on him!"

Even Xiao Yu's words did not shake Mu Long.

"Xiao Yu! What do girls know? The one who died was my beloved wife, not yours; of course you're not that hurt! Do you understand what it's like to lose a wife? I enjoy his downfall! It's nobody's business!"

Mu Long's eyes shone with pleasure and Xiao Yu didn't know how to respond.

Only Hiro, seeing his stubborn father, calmly replied.

"Father, what if I make it my business?"

Mu Long was stunned; he's always loved his son, but hearing him say such a thing took him by utter surprise.

"Hiro, you…"

Hiro calmly said, "Perhaps I should make things clear! These years, I have been cruel to Ying Ming, not because I hated him for mother's death, but because I promised mother I would help spur out his fighting spirit! I never had any reason to hate him! Now I have even less reason, because… For me he suffered cruelly at Sword Saint's hands. That is why his ability has been destroyed!"

"What?" Hearing Sword Saint's name, even Mu Long was shocked.

"You've… met Sword Saint?"

"Yes!" Hiro answered. "And he is much stronger than I had believed! He said that in three years hence, he will come again to duel with me!"

Mu Long said, "Since this trash has lost his martial arts abilities, then he won't be able to go in your place! He has no usefulness left; we don't need to keep him around anymore. I am throwing him out now!"

"Father!" Seeing his father approach the carriage as if to pull out Ying Ming, Hiro stepped in front of the carriage and stopped his father.

"Now Ying Ming is hurt and he needs someone to take care of him, if you want him to leave, then you have to kill me first!"

"You…" Hiro's sudden declaration stopped Mu Long.

But Hiro continued, "My life was saved by Ying Ming! That means his life is my life! I have promised to take care of him! I will repeat one more time, if you want him to leave, then you have to kill me first, otherwise I will be a faithless person denounced by the entire world!"

Who could predict this? Mu Long had always doted on his favored son. Now because of someone unrelated, their relationship was now sullied. How much love, hate, honor and trust is there?

With all the servants watching, Mu Long felt humiliated by his own son.

"How can you go against me for this useless trash?!" he roared. "You dare to go against me? All right, then I won't have a son like you!"

Shouting, Mu Long struck Hiro with a full-force palm strike. With a loud boom, Hiro was pushed back and blood streamed from the corner of his mouth, even a few of his teeth were knocked out. Mu Long is a palm technique expert!

But Hiro continued to stand proudly; for Ying Ming, he would not bend!

Ying Ming watched desperately from the carriage.

"Big… brother, forget about it! Just… let me leave here! I don't have any real value…"

Hearing that, Hiro instantly glared at Ying Ming.

"No! Brother, don't give in! You are too nice, and always relenting! Do you know, you can give in sometimes, but when you give too much, no one will respect you? We are men! We have to do what we think is right, and as long as it is the right thing we cannot back down! Not even half a step!"

Hiro glared back at his father Mu Long. Mu Long felt his heart wrung with pain, but it only angered him further.

"All right you little bastard! Then I won't hold back! Die!"

With that, Mu Long struck out ten more times, each one with all his strength. Loud booms rang through the air, and instantly, Hiro's proud face was covered with blood and welts!

But Hiro didn't make a single sound! To do what he thinks is right, to protect Ying Ming, he became a statue made of steel! A man of steel with a heart to match!

"Brother…Ying Ming…" Xiao Yu looked stunned, and her heart felt Hiro's pain. She cared not only for Ying Ming, but also for Hiro.

Mu Long hurt as well, he could not predict it would come to this with his son! He's already slapped Hiro forty to fifty times. Even his palms were aching, but his heart ached more…

Then suddenly Mu Long stopped.

All the servants, Hiro, Ying Ming and Xiao Yu were curious why Mu Long did not continue. Mu Long sighed towards the heavens.

"I'm… getting old…"

He paused and took a winded breath.

"I'm really getting old; I'm not as strong as I use to be! Ah…."

Yes! Mu Long was really old! In his heart he knew, every slap hurt his heart more! If it was ten years ago, he would have killed this ungrateful

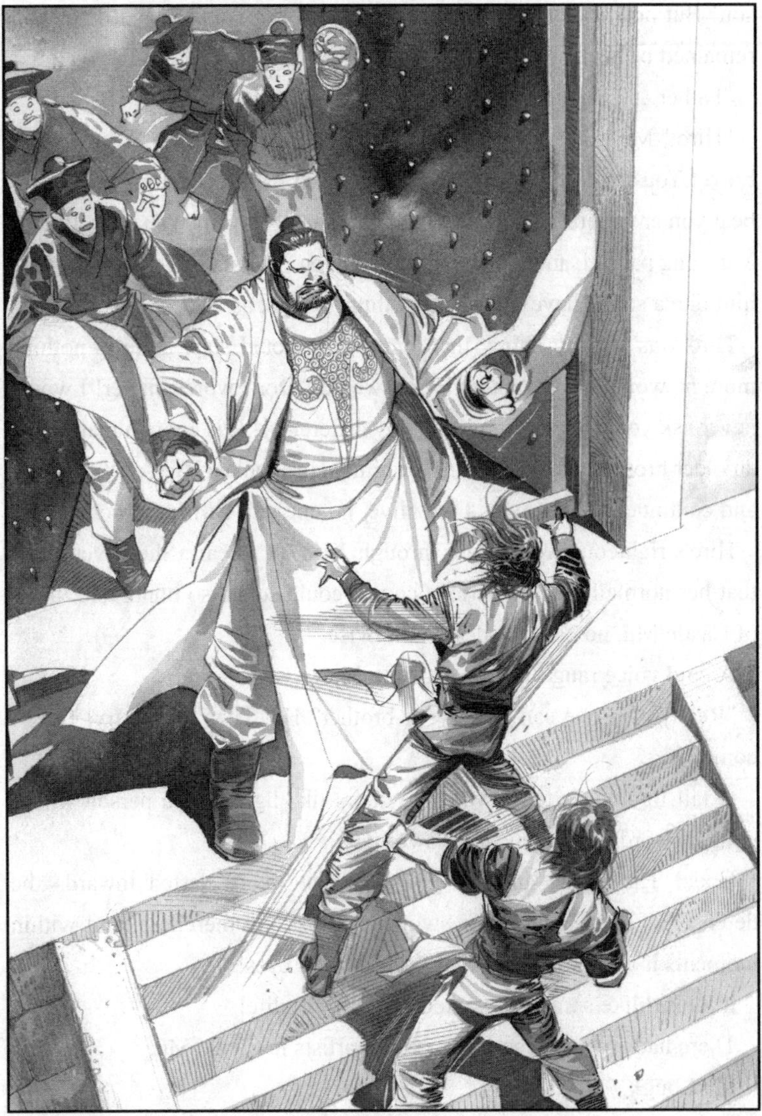

son! But now today, how can he dare kill him? This son that is all that remained of his beloved wife?

"Father…" Suddenly Hiro felt his father's pain.

"Hiro," Mu Long did not turn to look at him, and he said, "You are very brave! You are doing what you think is right! Father is getting old; I can't beat you any more! If you want that garbage to stay, then so be it. But…" Mu Long paused, and then continued, "Even if he stays, I will never treat him like a son! I have to do what I think is right as well!"

Hiro was already happy that Ying Ming could stay, there is nothing more he would have wanted. He answered, "Don't worry, father! I would never ask you to treat Ying Ming any differently! It is enough that he has an older brother like me to care for him!" Hiro looked back at Ying Ming and continued, "As long as I am alive, no one will harm my brother!"

Hiro's righteous words rang through Xiao Yu's heart. She never knew that her normally not-so-serious cousin could sound so honorable. In all of Castle Mu, no one dared say otherwise.

A cold voice rang outside of Castle Mu.

"Really? No one can harm your brother? Ha! Then let me try! Here I come!"

A tall figured darted toward the doors like lightning, a person with a golden sword! A golden snake sword!

Gods! The figure and the golden snake sword darted towards the defenseless Ying Ming! The sword was fast and merciless, and within moments it was poised between Ying Ming's eyes!

It looked like someone wanted Ying Ming's life!

There had always been three martial artists in Castle Mu.

Mu Long!

Hiro!

Ying Ming!

Now that Ying Ming's ability had been destroyed, there was only Mu Long and Hiro!

Where did this third person come from?

Where did this life-stealing golden snake sword come from?

Boom!

Just as the snake sword was inches away from Ying Ming, the blade tip was trapped between two fingers and instantly stopped!

But still the residual forced from the sword's stance made Ying Ming's head swim with dizziness. It was clearly someone using a powerful sword stance, but even more incredulous, the person who stopped the blade with his fingers was Hiro, who only had 5% of his power left!

Even with 5% of his powers, it was enough for Hiro to stop the blade? Looks like Hiro's strength far exceeded that of the attacker!

The owner of the snake sword did not press in for another try, and pulling back his sword he laughed.

"Haha! Great, what a great and honorable man! General Mu, your son Hiro's martial ability might quite possibly be on par with your own!"

The man holding the golden snake sword spoke with a foreign accent. Hiro, Ying Ming and Xiao Yu looked towards the speaker and saw a man in his twenties.

He was dressed as a scholar, with eyes of light brown. The corners of his eyes were clearly triangular and his nose was sharp like a hawk's. His hair was shiny black, and upon closer inspection, it seemed to have been dyed.

He gave off a weird aura, like someone not of this land.

When Hiro and the group stared at this young man, a high pitched, nasal voice called out laughing.

"Of course! Our general adores his son, so of course he would teach everything to him! It is not surprising that the son should surpass the father!"

The voice should belong to a woman, but the speaker was not female! Another person walked into Castle Mu, and it was an older man!

No, an older eunuch!

The eunuch looked to be around sixty years old, with a head full of white hair. His imitation of a woman's shy smile, made one's hair stand on end.

Where did this foreigner who tried to look like he belonged come from? And what about this man who was neither a man nor a woman?

Seeing these two, Hiro furrowed his brow and asked loudly, "Who are you? Why do you want to harm my brother?"

That old eunuch answered, "Hehe! Boy, you are so handsome when you are serious! Let me tell you, I am the head eunuch of the imperial palace, Eunuch Cao. This young master is a friend of your father's and I, Prince Jiu Luo!"

We have been guests at your home for over a day now. When we saw you defending your useless brother, Prince Jiu Luo just wanted to test if you were really a man of your word, and if you were strong enough to perform a 'task' for us!"

Task? Hiro's brows creased further, and Ying Ming was mystified.

Hiro asked, "Why do we have to perform this 'task' for you? What is this 'task'?"

Prince Jiu Luo who had not spoken up, laughed and said, "Hehe! So

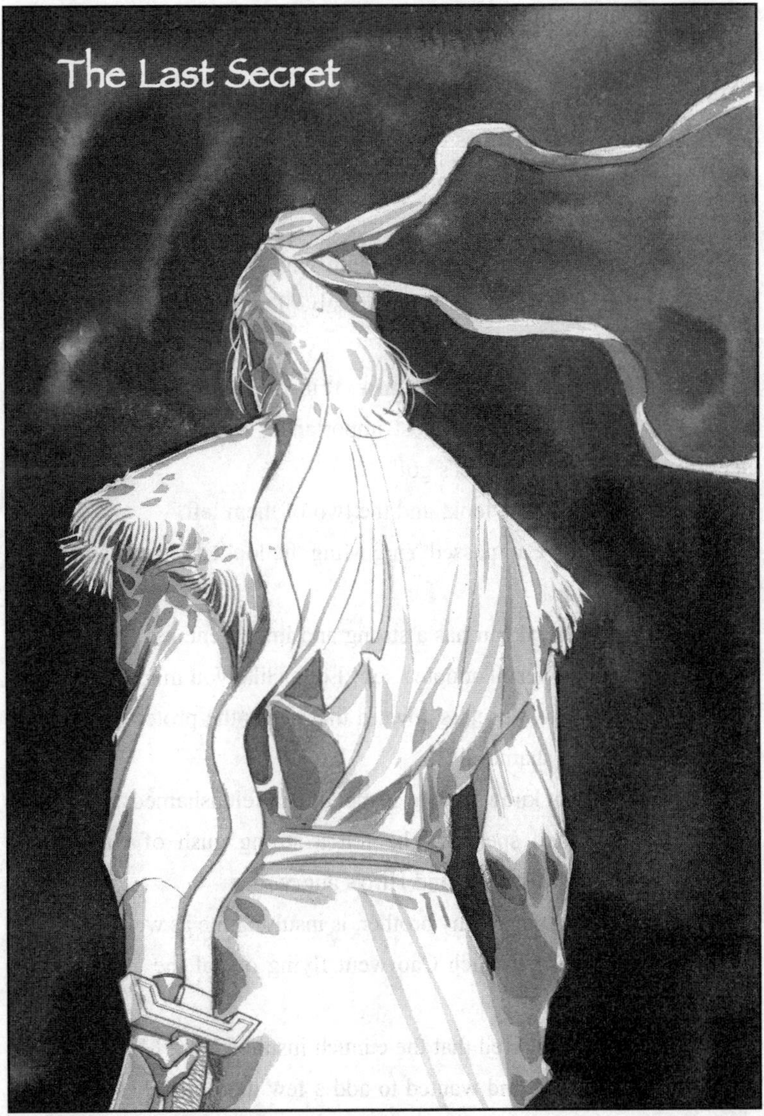
The Last Secret

your father hasn't told you? It's okay, we will let your father tell you in person!"

With a glance at Mu Long, he continued, "General Mu, I have tested your son and feel that he has enough power! But with his personality, it may not be possible for him to succeed! Perhaps there is something you can do to convince him?"

Mu Long seemed to have put his fight with his son behind him, and hearing the Prince's advice, he said earnestly, "I will! Prince Jiu Luo, don't worry!"

Having obtained Mu Long's promise, Prince Jiu Luo continued, "Very good! This is a task of the utmost importance; we're counting on you, General Mu! Eunuch Cao, let's go!"

He gave Eunuch Cao a look, and the two of them left.

But when Eunuch Cao passed Ying Ming, he looked him up and down and laughed.

"I heard that General Mu has a strong and intelligent son! He also has a lone star fated, powerful adopted son! Looks like you might really be a lone star, but you are a useless coward that needs the protection of your older brother! How shameful!"

Ying Ming did not know how to respond, and felt ashamed. But just as Eunuch Cao finished speaking, he felt a strong gush of chi rushing towards the back of his head, and Hiro's angry roar.

"Who ever dares to insult my brother, is insulting me as well! Get out!"

With a loud boom! Eunuch Cao went flying out of the gates like so much rubbish.

Hiro was greatly angered that the eunuch insulted Ying Ming's honor!

Hiro was still angry and wanted to add a few more punches, but Ying

Ming spoke up, "Big brother, just forget it! He's our father's friend, don't do it just for me…"

Before he could finish, another force grasped Hiro's hands. Mu Long finally stepped in.

"Hiro! Eunuch Cao is a high ranking government official, don't be so impetuous!"

Hiro argued, "But he was so rude to Ying Ming!"

"He merely insulted a dog, it's no big deal! Hiro, I have compromised on several issues with you today. Let this go and we'll call it even!"

With that, Hiro felt if he continued to harass Eunuch Cao, Mu Long might treat Ying Ming worse, so he gave in.

Eunuch Cao crawled back up from the ground and protested to Prince Jiu Luo.

"Ahaha… Prince Jiu Luo, Hiro hit me, your most loyal servant! You have to uphold the justice!" With that he began throwing a tantrum that even the Prince looked down upon.

"You should be beat! Because you forgot one thing!"

"What?"

"Never insult a man, even a useless man; you have to fight him with your real power! This is the rule of the game between real men!" Prince Jiu Luo looked towards Hiro, and asked, "Hiro, don't you think so? Hehe…"

Hiro made no answer, merely standing like a hawk protecting Ying Ming. Prince Jiu Luo quickly grew bored and made his formal farewell to Mu Long.

"General Mu! Remember what we talked about! Convince your son! Eunuch Cao and I will be going now!"

He left with Eunuch Cao in tow.

Strangely, Prince Jiu Luo's command instantly made Eunuch Cao stop his crying and whining! Eunuch Cao was a powerful official, so what made him so obedient to Prince Jiu Luo's commands? Almost like a trained dog? A loyal dog following its master's every whim?

Who is this Prince Jiu Luo?

As Hiro, Ying Ming and Xiao Yu thought of this, Mu Long turned to Hiro.

"Hiro, follow me! I have something important to tell you!"

Mu Long sounded so mysterious, not at all like his normal self! Hiro followed his father into the study, and he finally understood his secrecy!

A terrible secret that he did not want to believe...

The first thing Mu Long did was to close the doors securely, then he turned and faced Hiro.

"Hiro, as you know I have been a top ranked general for many years in court," carefully he told him. "Why do you think I suddenly retired in the prime of my life?"

Hiro had always wondered, and in fact everyone in Castle Mu had wondered for many years. General Mu was not very old, yet he had already returned home.

Hearing his father mention this age-old conundrum, Hiro's palms began to sweat, because he knew a shocking explanation was to follow.

Mu Long smiled bitterly, and answered, "Hiro, my son, do you know? I had to retire before my time, because the Emperor discovered that I..." he paused, choking on his words. "I was consorting with the Jin!"

*[Translator's Note: China's history is well documented with conquests by outside "barbaric" tribes. The Jin was one such tribe, another famous one*

*like the Mongolians who took over China and formed the Yuan Dynasty. Later the Manchus took over and formed the last dynasty in Chinese history, the Qing. Consorting with these tribes was considered high treason and punishable by death!]*

Consorting with the Jin? Hiro was shocked! China had always been at war with these outside invading tribes. Even ordinary citizens were loyal when it came to dealing with the Jin. Mu Long was a famed general. How could he consort with the Jin? And the Emperor was suspicious?

This was almost impossible to believe.

Hiro asked dumbly, "You consorted with the Jin, and the Emperor began to suspect. You decided to act first, so you quit your position and retired?"

Mu Long nodded slowly, admitting the truth.

"But why did you consort with the Jin?"

"Because," Mu Long sighed, "I had conceived of a plan long ago with the Jin to take over China. That Prince Jiu Luo you just met, he was the prince of Jin. He has snuck into China to contact our spy in the imperial court, Eunuch Cao. Also, three years hence, he will initiate his major plan and needs our help. He wanted to see if you were the right candidate for the job! These past ten years, though I have retired, I kept in touch with the Jin."

Hiro listened silently, but his heart sank to the lowest depths of hell! No wonder General Mu had been so busy after Madame Mu's death; he didn't even have time to visit her grave! This year he didn't go, because of his important meetings with Prince Jiu Luo and Eunuch Cao!

Hiro suddenly understood, although he had always been upset with his father for the way he treated Ying Ming, he still always respected his father for being a patriot and general who shed his blood protecting his country. He had always been proud to be the son of a veteran, but now everything had changed, it was all ashes and dust, blown away with the wind...

He could not hide his great disappointment, and righteously he asked his father, "Father! Do you know what you are doing? You are a traitor! Are you planning to sell all the good people of China to the Jin?"

"Is that really so?" Mu Long smiled bitterly once more, and said, "Hiro, are you sure that I am a traitor? Do you know, consorting with Jiu Luo and others, I am not actually betraying my country, just the opposite..."

He paused at looked deeply into Hiro's eyes.

"I am saving my country!"

Saving his country? Hiro laughed coldly! For the first time, he discovered how truly shameless his father was! He called this *saving* his country? Hiro laughed again.

"Saving your country? Are you joking?"

"Do I look like I am joking?" Mu Long was serious, he didn't look to be joking.

"Hiro, let me tell you another secret. After you hear this secret, you will understand that I have never betrayed my country!"

"What secret?"

"A final secret that you might not believe!" Mu Long added with a mysterious smile, and then he finally spoke.

Hiro was shocked to the core!

Not only shocked, but it seemed all his blood froze in place!

He lost his initial anger towards his father, and his extremities felt frozen, the sweat drops on his palms freezing one by one! It was a secret he did not want to believe!

"No... It's not possible! It's not possible! It was not possible!"

Hiro stammered, "This secret... it can't be true, it's not true! How could you not be betraying your country? You are... saving it? You...? You... AHHHH..."

Hiro lost his composure and screamed in anguish! What kind of secret would make even the calm Hiro scream so?

The scream not only shook the whole study, but also shook Ying Ming and Xiao Yu waiting outside!

Ying Ming and Xiao Yu could not believe the scream came from Hiro's mouth! It sounded so desperate, like he had just heard the worst thing in the entire world!

Xiao Yu asked anxiously, "Brother Ying Ming, why did Brother Hiro scream like that? Is he fighting with Uncle Mu Long again? Have they come to blows?"

Ying Ming made no answers, because he understood, Hiro must have found out something which he could not hope to change or escape, something that he did not know how to deal with!

After Hiro's outburst, the study fell deathly silent. Like a faithful son, whose heart had died... A man who lost heart in himself...

The silence lasted long moments until finally a bang issued from the door. Hiro finally emerged slowly from the study with a pale face -- a face white as a sheet. He was clearly in shock. Mu Long walked out of the study with him and said, "Hiro, thinking about what I am asking you to do three years from now..."

Not waiting for his father to finish, Hiro answered firmly, "There's no need to think further!"

"Father, even though you have told me this final secret, there are some things I will never do! If you want it done, then find someone else!"

"Hiro..." Mu Long wanted to say something more, but Hiro had already stepped away to join Ying Ming and Xiao Yu, he never turning once to look at his father!

Mu Long shook his head in defeat, and finally turned back to his study.

Xiao Yu quickly asked in curiosity, "Brother Hiro, what is this 'final secret'?"

Hiro smiled with infinite bitterness, and his words were filled with sorrow.

"Since it's a secret, it's better if no one knows of it! Sister Xiao Yu, do you think that I would so easily disclose a secret? You must be overestimating your attractiveness!"

Hiro's anger made his words seem more cruel than usual. Xiao Yu was stunned and red in the face, she didn't dare ask again!

Hiro knew he said too much, but it was too late now -- all had been said. Only the silent Ying Ming stood by, because he knew that there must be a reason Hiro was hiding the truth. He didn't want to force Hiro to tell them, so he just said, "Big Brother, I know it must be something difficult to face."

"Since you don't want to tell us, we won't force you. I just want you to know something. No matter what kind of problem you are facing, Xiao Yu and I will always be by your side. We will face it together!"

Hearing Ying Ming's words, Hiro was greatly touched! Yes, no matter how terrible the problems, he knew that Ying Ming and Xiao Yu would be by his side. But there were some things in this world that were not so easy; things that were impossible to resolve...

"Thank you, brother!" Hiro suddenly said. "But the world is getting more complex! So complicated that even the three of us together might not be able to face it! Some things I wish I never knew!" Hiro seemed to be hinting at something.

"But no matter what happens, the three of us will always be together! So let's celebrate our time together! As for those things that must eventually be dealt with, we will face them in time, right? Hahaha..."

Hiro suddenly laughed out loud, and the cloud of despair surrounding his face instantly disappeared. He's returned to his normal, calm, cheerful self.

No one wanted to face these unsavory truths! Just let them disappear with the wind!

It is better to enjoy the happiness of each moment to its fullest!

Who can predict the troubles of tomorrow? Because of that, one should enjoy the present all the more...

In the days following, Hiro seemed to have forgotten the unhappiness of his father's great secret.

Even Mu Long seemed more subdued, he did not insist on Hiro helping him with the mysterious tasks that must be accomplished in three years. He seemed to respect Hiro's decision.

That Prince Jiu Luo and Eunuch Cao never appeared in the Castle again.

Since finding out the final secret, Hiro had grown to be wary of his father. He did not tell Mu Long that they had the Hero Swords, he just hid them, to prevent any unwanted problems.

Everything seemed normal, as if nothing happened.

Ying Ming recovered as best he could, with no martial arts ability left. But in his heart he knew that he was not as he once was.

For example, after he recovered, Ying Ming attempted to clean his own room. He did not want to trouble anyone else with these trivial tasks. He had always done these chores himself.

He thought himself more than able, but he could barely finish straightening half the room. Exhaustion racked his body and every muscle felt cramped and strained.

Now that he had lost his martial arts ability, he was less capable than an ordinary person!

But no servant in Castle Mu had ever cared for this long neglected son. Even when Hiro forced someone to come, they only did the bare minimum and then left.

Finally Xiao Yu and Hiro stepped in to personally care for Ying Ming.

Xiao Yu was a kind girl and had always felt a strange attraction to Ying Ming. She would be happy to do anything for him, even if her sister Chiu Hong thought it foolish.

Hiro was even more admirable, he did all the chores without any complaint. He would roll up his sleeves each time and work diligently at all the chores. Even if his pure white-robes were soiled, he didn't seem to mind. His martial arts ability enabled him to finish his tasks quicker than Xiao Yu, but sadly his skills were wasted on these menial tasks.

But Hiro never seemed the least bit tired or upset. He was hoping to make Ying Ming's life just a little better with each day. Even if this life was ordinary, it was what Ying Ming wished for, and Hiro respected his wish.

There were several times when Ying Ming became ill because he no longer had chi to protect himself. He was feverish for five days and nights. Xiao Yu remained awake for three full days to care for him, but in the end she fell asleep as well, only Hiro...

He is always there.

While Ying Ming was sick, he stayed by his brother's side for all five days. He never seemed to get tired, and always stayed by Ying Ming's side -- faithfully taking care of him. He never rested for a moment, not even half a second!

What can make this hot blooded man so unyielding? Perhaps he cherished his brother's heart...

Ying Ming was born with high hopes from his mother. But he possessed a lone star luck; he was an unlucky person that everyone avoided. In his short sixteen years of life, he had never experienced any warmth. But now with the loss of his martial arts ability, Hiro had been taking care of him. Hiro wanted to do everything he could to make Ying Ming's life a little happier.

But his hard work and his honor seemed crazy in the eyes of his father and Xiao Yu's sister Chiu Hong.

All the maids laughed at Hiro behind his back.

*Why would Hiro give up the good life to take care of that unlucky lone star? Hehe... doing work for such an unlucky person, even we do not want to do! Master Hiro has gone crazy. He must owe something to that lone star in another life, or else why would he be so good to him?*

No one understood why Hiro treated Ying Ming so well. They didn't understand, because they had never experienced the depth of feeling that Hiro and Ying Ming shared... Hiro will never be able to repay Ying Ming for everything he had done. And Ying Ming will never be able to repay everything Hiro had done!

Though the maids dare not make fun of Hiro to his face, Ying Ming heard their words, and he felt sad for his brother.

He knew that the easiest way for him to stop their cruel words was for him to leave Castle Mu!

If he left Castle Mu then all the gossip would disappear along with him!

Since he had already become useless, lingering would only force Hiro to care for him for the rest of his life. He would become Hiro's lifelong burden! He didn't want Hiro to waste away his life for a useless person like himself, so he decided to leave!

Ying Ming did not hesitate, in the middle of the night, when everyone slept, he gathered his meager belongs and snuck out of the Castle.

He kept walking! No matter how tired, Ying Ming had to keep going! He felt that Hiro had suffered too much for him...

But not far outside of Castle Mu, he stoped. There stood a person near a tree, with both hands behind his back, staring intently at Ying Ming.

It was Hiro!

Hiro flashed his usual smile and said, "Ying Ming."

He looked intently at him. "Are you running away? Are you abandoning your big brother?"

"Big... Brother?" Ying Ming knew his secret was out when he saw Hiro. His brother was smart enough to anticipate that he would try to leave, and waited here all along. Ying Ming tried to explain, "I am not abandoning you! In fact, I have never been able to repay your kindness!"

Hiro smiled bitterly and said, "I want to be nice to you... Do you think I am expecting you to repay me?"

"But…" Ying Ming said, "I already owe you so much, do you know that all the maids in Castle Mu are making fun of you? They said you are wasting your time on trash like me. I wanted to leave Castle Mu. Perhaps it would make things a little better… It's the only way to resolve the problem!"

Hiro said, "It is not the only way! There is another way you can make them stop mocking me!"

"What is that?"

"That is…" Hiro never even batted an eye, saying calmly, "If I go with you!"

Hiro's words greatly shocked Ying Ming. Stunned he asked, "But you can't do that! Big brother, Castle Mu is wealthy and powerful, you will have a great future if you stay here. Why, for me, are you willing to give up a wonderful future? I will be a heavy burden to you! I will cause you trouble!"

Hearing that Hiro was still unmoved, full of hidden meaning, he answered, "You've already caused me trouble!"

Since Ying Ming lost his martial ability to save Hiro, Hiro had vowed to care for Ying Ming; he'd already decided.

"But," Hiro spoke once more, "so what if you cause me trouble? If you were ready to leave Castle Mu alone, and I did not know where you went, I would never be able to rest easy! If you don't want me to worry then let me leave this place with you!"

"But brother, you did not say goodbye to father...!" Ying Ming wanted to argue further, but Hiro cut him off.

"Don't worry! I already left a note for him! He will know that we are gone when he wakes in the morning, you'll see! I've even brought the Hero Swords along!"

With that, Hiro extended the hands he'd been hiding behind his back. Revealed were the two Hero Swords! It seemed that he'd long decided to leave Castle Mu! For Ying Ming, he easily made this decision.

But Ying Ming still tried to convince him.

"But Big Brother, do you really want to abandon father?"

Hiro seemed to have some regrets.

"Yes, I don't want to leave father behind! But I don't want to leave you either! He has plenty of people to take care of him, but you, you only have one big brother!"

Ying Ming had nothing left! No parents! No marital ability! He was all alone, but now at least he had a big brother like Hiro…

"Besides," Hiro said, "ever since I found out about the secret, I have not wanted to stay in Castle Mu any longer. I wanted to leave here anyway, so this is a good thing… Ying Ming, if you still think of me as your big brother, then you will do as I say and let me leave this place with you. Let's forget about this place, and start a new life!"

Start a new life?

Yes! Only by leaving behind the unhappy memories of Mu Town would the two brothers be able to start again. Ying Ming knew that Hiro meant every word, there was no use trying to convince him, otherwise Hiro would not be such a great big brother!

He finally nodded.

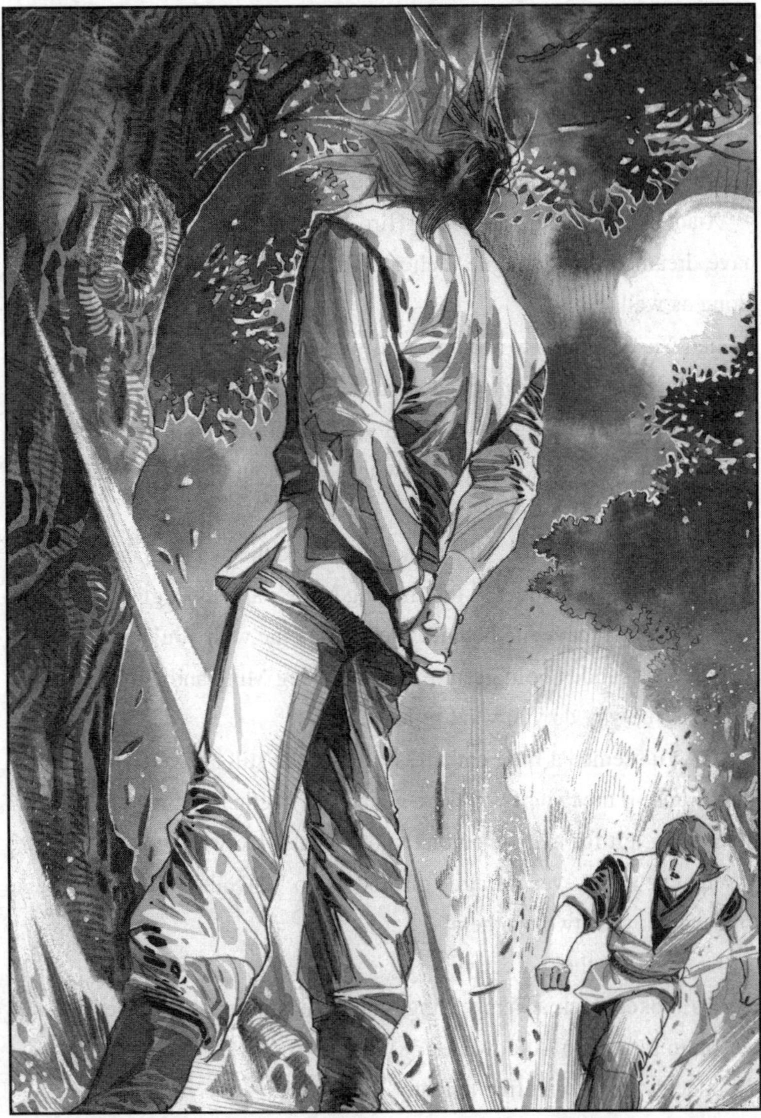

Seeing Ying Ming agree, Hiro smiled in happiness.

"That's my good brother! Let's hurry and leave this god-forsaken place!"

Just as he was about to leave with Ying Ming, he turned to see a slim figure standing by another tree, watching them wistfully!

"Xiao… Yu?" Ying Ming and Hiro said together. They would never have dreamed that a fragile, delicate girl like her would have followed along as well.

Xiao Yu continued to look wistfully at the two brothers, with a light smile she said, "You're shocked right?"

"You wouldn't have guessed that I wanted to leave with you?"

Hiro sighed, "Yes, we didn't know that you would find out and want to come along."

"Since I'm here then…" She turned and faced the two brothers. Walking towards them, she suddenly fell in Ying Ming's arms, begging.

"Please don't leave me behind! Please take me with you!"

Xiao Yu's sudden bold gesture shocked Ying Ming and Hiro.

"Xiao Yu, why do you want to leave?"

Xiao Yu seemed a little embarrassed, but she still answered honestly.

"Because if the two of you were gone from Castle Mu, then there would be nothing left for me! I wouldn't know what to do with myself!"

Who knew that even a fragile girl like Xiao Yu would have the courage to leave with the two brothers!

She cared for them greatly!

Hiro looked back at Ying Ming, and both brothers knew they had no reason to turn Xiao Yu down.

Suddenly Hiro's carefree laughter rang out.

"Very well then, if you are not afraid of living a peasant's life, and cooking for us, then we would love for you to come!"

Xiao Yu was overjoyed that Hiro agreed, and laughed.

"Don't worry! I will do my best to fix you the best food… If you don't mind being poisoned…"

With that Hiro laughed too, and even Ying Ming smiled deeply.

He looked at Hiro and then back at Xiao Yu, and in their kind faces he discovered that he was the luckiest person after all.

But that moment of togetherness, that moment of laughter, that moment of truth, that moment of happiness…

How long would it last in his sorrow filled life?

A fiery phoenix, whose heart had died, whose wings had been broken...

An eagle that should be soaring, but has vowed to stay behind and protect the phoenix...

And a lonely sparrow.

Phoenix, eagle and sparrow, wanting to live together, in the wide world, wherever will they rest?

Where can they stay?

Three months later, at the end of the year.

December.

In a small nameless village...

Inside a small nameless hut…

The small hut was filled with swords.

Wooden replicas of the Hero Sword!

Hiro looked at the wooden Hero Swords filling the hut and smiled.

The hut he currently resided in was a small tiny stone chamber. It was old, with only two small bedroom chambers and a smaller living room, which was already filled with knickknacks and replicas of the Hero Sword. The conditions were poor.

The small hut could not compare to the luxury and beauty of Castle Mu. It was like comparing heaven and hell!

But Hiro did not seem to mind, and his face shone with contentment, because the small hut he shared with Ying Ming and Xiao Yu. And he hoped that it would always be their home!

Thinking back to three months ago when he, Ying Ming and Xiao Yu left Castle Mu, they continued going forward. They didn't know where they were going, they just knew that they had to leave Castle Mu, and go as far as possible.

Finally, after countless days, countless miles, the three settled down in a small, nameless village. This village was too small to even warrant a name. But this was exactly what Hiro and Ying Ming wanted.

With some remaining silver, Hiro rented a small hut and purchased some simple household goods, and settled here. The hut was very small. Hiro and Ying Ming shared one bedroom, while Xiao Yu took the other one. But there was one good thing about living in the village: no one knew of their past! No one knew that Hiro was the son of the famous General Mu Long, and no one knew that Ying Ming was the fearsome, unlucky lone star of Mu Town!

The three of them could start over anew!

It was all worth it to leave Castle Mu and begin again!

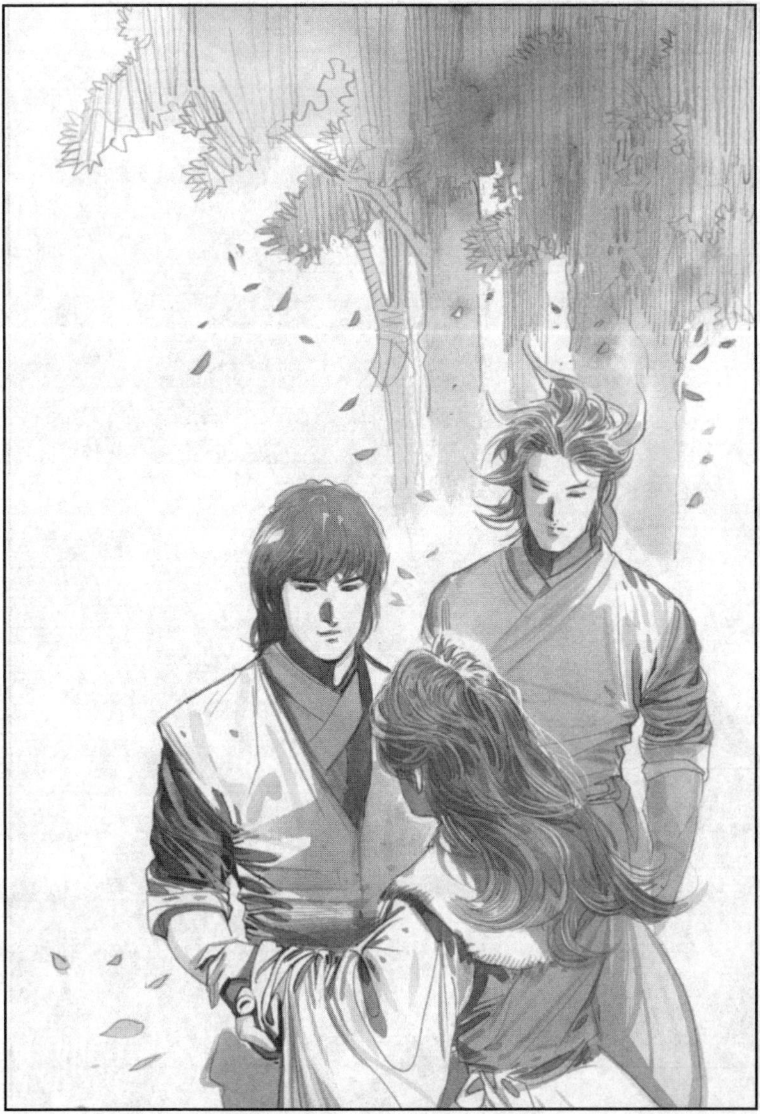

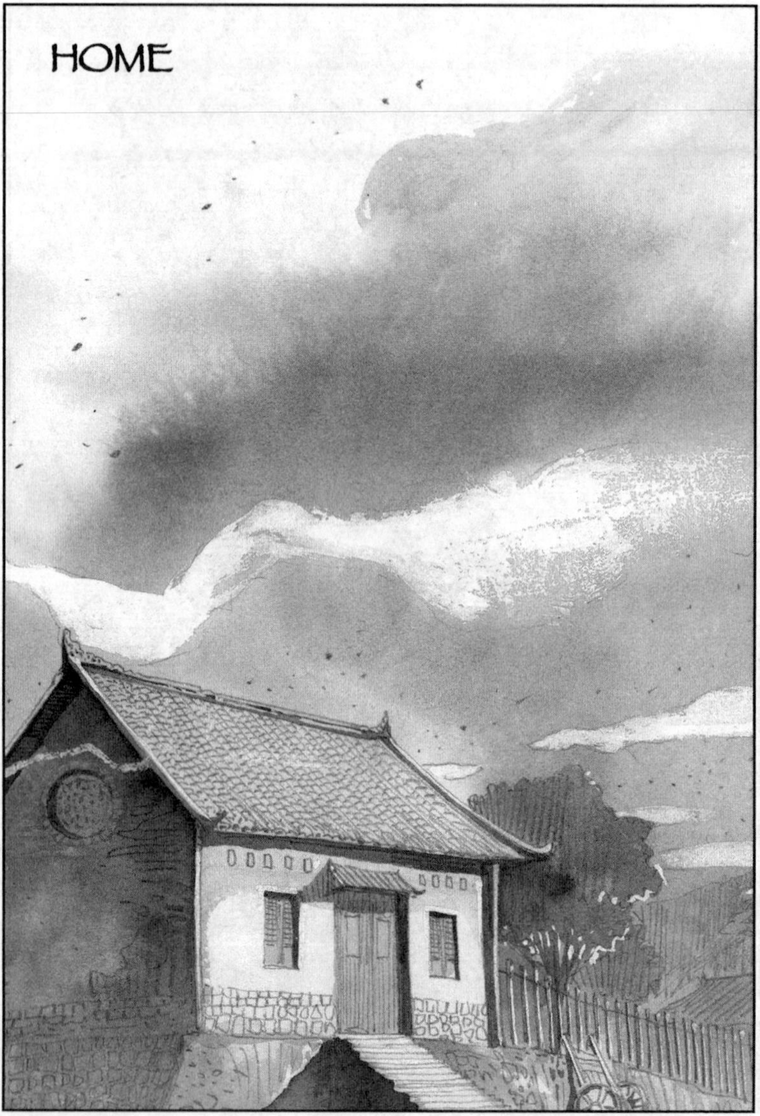
HOME

The neighbors thought that they were siblings, two brothers and their sister. The brothers were just and polite, while the sister was kind and warm. The harmonious little family was quite the envy of many villagers.

The only regret in their eyes was that Ying Ming's health was not so good. He often succumbed to illness, but his older brother and sister would always stay up as long as needed to care for him. Under their tender care, he always regained his health!

The three of them had already used up Hiro's last remaining silvers, and the time came for them to do something to make a living!

For more money, Hiro traveled around the village and performed martial arts feats for money.

For a nobleman's son such as Hiro to do such a thing was sad and degrading.

But Hiro never complained, for it was all worthwhile in his eyes.

So Hiro worked hard everyday to make a living, but was it enough for him to work alone? Finally Xiao Yu had to join him and sing along side and Ying Ming...

To survive, and to prove that he could indeed help while Hiro did martial arts and Xiao Yu sang, he learned to play the erhu!

It seemed that he had a natural talent for the stringed instrument, and might be just as talented with the erhu as he once was with the sword. His ability grew with each passing day.

Then he developed his own style of play. The erhu he played sounded mournful and lonely, filled with endless sorrow, entrancing all the villages with its sad song.

From then on, Ying Ming fell in "love" with the erhu!

*This is better!* Hiro thought so, since Ying Ming would never be able to wield the Hero Sword. for if he could not "love" his sword, then he could "love" his erhu. That was a good thing as well! At least Ying Ming wouldn't feel so useless!

On the surface, Hiro agreed that Ying Ming should learn the erhu, but what did he really think?

Perhaps somewhere deep in his heart, he still held out the smallest speck of hope, that one day the phoenix that dived into the flames would be reborn; the legendary heaven sword would once again wield the Hero Sword…

But his hope would only stifle Ying Ming, and make him feel pressured. So Hiro hid his hopes deep in his heart, and buried the Hero Sword in the yard outside their small hut.

But when he came home from work, he could not forget the Hero Swords. Sometimes when he was bored at night, he would carve wooden pieces into the shape of the Hero Sword. Slowly, the small hut filled up with big and small carvings of the Hero Sword.

Much like tonight…

Tonight the stars shone especially bright, because today was a good day.

It was New Year's Eve.

Tomorrow would be a new year.

This was the first New Year for Hiro, Ying Ming and Xiao Yu, and the first new year since they left Castle Mu. To celebrate, the three decided to not work for the day and prepared for New Year festivities.

Ying Ming and Xiao Yu were planning to buy some cakes and vegetables from the market, so they left early. Hiro was the only one left, so he cleaned the rooms and put up a new calligraphy sign to usher in the coming of spring.

But Hiro's calligraphy was not filled with the usual wish for wealth -- he wrote, "Harmoniously Together", "Peace for the Home".

For someone who once had everything, money is nothing. He did not mind living this simple life. His only wish was for the three of them to live here always in harmony, together. Most importantly, he wished for Ying Ming and Xiao Yu's safety.

Lastly, Hiro did not forget to write one last line, "Always striving for betterment".

Who does he want to strive for betterment?

After writing the calligraphy, it was still early, so Hiro took out some wood and began once again to carve. Of course it was the Hero Sword.

He carved and carved, and forgot all about time. When he finished carving a brand new Hero Sword, he discovered that it had already become dark, and Ying Ming and Xiao Yu had not returned.

Hiro began to worry.

"It's so late already! Why are Ying Ming and Xiao Yu still not back? They just went to buy some treats from the market, why are they gone for so long? Did something happen?"

Hiro tried to reassure himself, "No, it's nothing like that. Perhaps they just got excited because it was the New Year and decided to play a while longer in the market! Yes, I gave them a little bit of New Year's money and told them to buy new clothes. That must be what they were doing!"

Thinking of the New Year's money, Hiro smiled bitterly.

They have been living from day to day, where did he get New Year's money? This New Year's money was actually from selling his white robes to Rich Man Gu in the village.

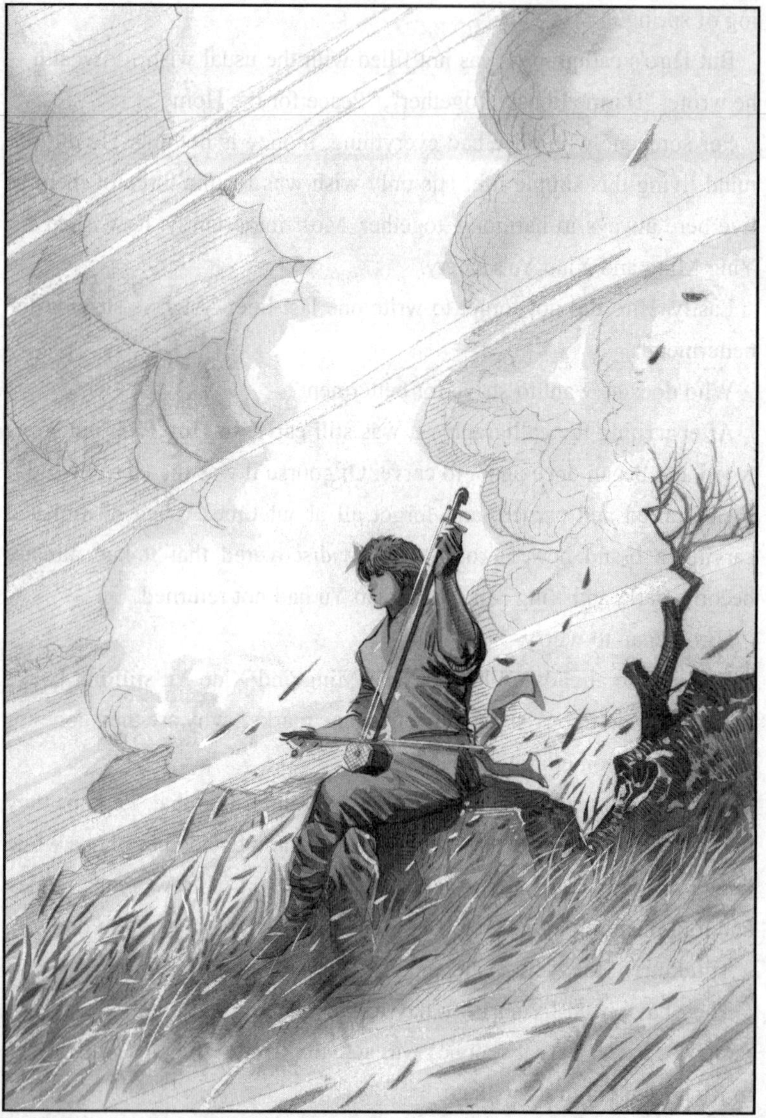

Hiro's white robe was extremely well-made, sewn from real silk and exceedingly precious. Hiro had only left Castle Mu for one month, so his white robe was still new. If he wanted to sell it, someone would surely want to buy it.

Hiro could have worn his white robe for the New Year, but he had already grown use to his rough homespun. He didn't care to wear anything new. Most importantly, Ying Ming and Xiao Yu's clothes were even worse than his. He hoped that they could wear something nice as well, so without hesitation he sold his white robe!

That robe was a birthday present from his father, Mu Long, when he turned 16…

Time slowly passed by, but Ying Ming and Xiao Yu still did not return. Now Hiro really began to worry.

"Something's… wrong, even if they walked to the farthest clothes shop, they should be back by now! What happened to them? No, I shouldn't worry so much! Although Ying Ming can no longer use martial arts, Xiao Yu is with him, so nothing will happen!"

Yes, no matter where Ying Ming went, Xiao Yu was never far behind…

If a girl felt something from a boy, then she would always want to be by his side, right? And care for him?

Hiro understood Xiao Yu's heart, and he smiled bitterly once more.

Xiao Yu's heart went out to Ying Ming, but what about Hiro's heart for Xiao Yu?

In these past days, Hiro didn't know when it started, but he began to feel something special for Xiao Yu. Even in his dreams, he began to see her smiling face and hear her warm voice.

But Xiao Yu always kept this distance between them, although she was never far. Xiao Yu always stayed close to Ying Ming though.

Even those who are the most dense can see who is in her heart.

Of course, Hiro sometimes felt awkward, but he was never jealous of Ying Ming. He understood more than anyone that some things just cannot be forced.

If Ying Ming were really to accept Xiao Yu's love for him, then as the big brother he would feel happy for him. So Hiro always buried his feelings for Xiao Yu in the deepest, darkest corner of his heart...

Hiro was lost in thought, and continued carving the Hero Sword, when suddenly the wood snapped in half and the wooden Hero Sword broke!

A broken Sword!

Hiro stopped.

"Oh no, it's just a wooden Hero Sword, and it is so late, it broke at such a time, this is... A bad omen? Did something bad happen? Am I... thinking too seriously?"

No! He was not, at the same time his sword broke, there was a pounding at his door!

Hiro rushed to the front door, but it was not Ying Ming and Xiao Yu standing outside, rather a man he met while doing martial arts in the village "Dumb Head the Third"!

"It's terrible! Hiro, it's... terrible!" Third seemed lost, and seeing Hiro he could barely catch his breath.

With Third in such a panicked state, Hiro knew something was wrong.

"Third! Calm down! Tell me! What happened?"

Third swallowed a deep breath and began.

"Hiro, your brother... on the street... Something bad happened!"

Something bad happened! Hiro stood as if struck by lightning!

Hiro could not have predicted Ying Ming's fate would be so bad, even after he lost his martial arts.

"Third… what happened? My brother… how is he?" Hiro didn't know what to do.

"Hiro, I heard that you sold your expensive white robe to Rich Man Gu to get New Year's money for your brother and sister. But your brother and sister did not want to see you wearing your old homespun for New Years. They said that your father gave it to you and it meant a lot, so… your brother and sister went to Rich Man Gu hoping to give back the money and get your robe back…

"But Rich Man Gu was so mean! He said that you sold it to him fair and square, and was not willing to give it back; unless they gave back the money and your brother also work as his servant for a whole day!"

Third paused for a moment to catch his breath. He continued, "Rich Man Gu knew that your brother's health was not so good; he was just giving them a hard time! But your brother agreed without even thinking about it! Why did he want to get the white robe back so badly?"

Third didn't understand, but Hiro did. Ying Ming insisted on getting the garment, because Hiro would be so happy to see that the two of them cared so much for him. He didn't care about Gu's demands! Thinking of that Hiro was deeply touched.

"Ying Ming, Ying Ming, you're much too…" Hiro thought in his heart, but he asked, "Then if Ying Ming agreed to be his servant, what else could have happened?"

"Rich Man Gu didn't think your brother, being so sickly, would agree so quickly. You know how those rich folk like torturing us poor folks. He wouldn't allow your sister Xiao Yu to help him, and forced your brother to draw twenty buckets of water from the well! Ah, even the strongest villager here can't pull twenty buckets of water! And your brother in his condition...?"

"Then what happened?" Hiro worried even more.

"You wouldn't believe it!" Third reminisced, "I thought your brother wouldn't even be able to pull up one bucket! But he clenched his teeth and endured the pain, until finally he drew twenty buckets of water; but by that time blood was dripping from his mouth and he was clearly exhausted. We all knew how hard he worked! We all thought that Rich Man Gu would give back the white robe, but he said he had no intention of giving it back. He said it was all a joke and he kicked your brother and sister out!"

"What?" Hiro's anger flared as he listened.

"Yeah! Your brother and sister didn't leave of course. Rich Man Gu sent more than twenty of his vicious dogs after your brother and sister!"

Hiro's heart tightened even further. Third slowed his pace and continued more calmly. "Your brother was already all worn out. He could barely stand, but to protect her, he forced himself up. In the end, your brother was bitten all over by the dogs, and..."

When a dragon returns to the sea, he is mocked by brine, while a tiger returns to the hill to be mocked by hounds. Hearing this, Hiro could no longer control himself -- it was just to get back a set of robes. He didn't need to be anyone's servant or slave -- to be made fun of, or to be abused by their dogs...! Ying Ming already lost his martial arts skills. This was terrible...

"Ying Ming!"

With the fastest lightfoot speed, Hiro rushed out like a bolt of lightning!

Third was stunned! Hiro always performed the most ordinary martial arts feats in the village square, so he never dreamed that in an instant Hiro could disappear from his line of sight!

"Ah…"

Third exclaimed, "Hiro is such a scary person? He's so powerful… in martial arts? Then why does he live with his brother and sister in this poor village? Who is he suffering for? Who?"

Perhaps Hiro was the only one who knew the answer!

He was doing this for a phoenix!

A dead phoenix!


The village was not so big, and Hiro's lightfoot was swift!

In less than five minutes, Hiro had already sprinted through the streets!

Upon arrival, he saw something unforgettable!

There was a crowd gathered in front of Rich Man Gu's house. They were not a bunch of gossiping villagers; these villagers were fighting and shouting!

Yes, all the villagers were angered by this familiar scene of the rich oppressing the poor!

They were shouting and fighting with the twenty dogs in front of Rich Man Gu's house, because the dogs were attacking two people...

Ying Ming and Xiao Yu!

The dogs continually leapt at the brother and sister, who were trapped in their midst. Although Ying Ming was exhausted, he continued to wave a sword-like stick in his hands, trying his best to protect Xiao Yu standing behind him!

Hiro could tell that Ying Ming's swings were sword techniques! Although he lost his chi, his talent for the sword was still amazing. He was able to beat back some of the dogs! But still many were not scared away by the stick; they rushed forward and Ying Ming's body showed several wounds where he had been bitten -- some with chunks of flesh completely torn away!

But no matter how hurt, Ying Ming stood his ground to protect Xiao Yu -- and with luck, maybe he could get back that precious white robe, the one he wanted to give to Hiro!

The villagers wanted to help, but each of the dogs was as big as a small bull, taller than the biggest villager.

But the unrepentant Rich Man Gu laughed with his hands on his waist.

"Hehe! Go ahead and shout! You can't help him! You're too scared to help him! He's pretty good, he looks so sickly, but he's able to fend off my dogs! But look at him, he's already wounded, he won't last that long! You're all witnesses; it's not me that killed him; some dogs bit him to death! Ah! If you kill, you have to pay with your life! But if a dog kills, then the dog must pay! It's none of my business, even if you brought the case to a magistrate, I am innocent!"

How shameless! They were clearly his dogs, but he still claimed innocence. Many of the villagers were so angry, they thought to jump in and help, but they barely walked in a few steps before they were bitten and hurt by the vicious hounds!

"Haha! See? Who else wants to try? You shouldn't just stand around, you should help him! Hehe, I should be merciful and end it right here!"

There are always those small-minded, petty individuals everywhere who enjoy oppressing others. Rich Man Gu laughed cruelly, and with a whistle, ordered his dogs to attack at once! All twenty of them leapt towards Ying Ming!

Ying Ming could do nothing! He was already hurt from the numerous bite wounds, and he barely had any strength left. But there was always someone, who would save him at the most critical moment.

With a thunderous boom, like a immortal descending from the heavens, a man fell like lightning amidst the dogs and roared.

"Beasts! You want to kill my brother? You are not good enough! I will slay you all!"

Anger! Hatred! Pain!

When hero saw Ying Ming being bitten by the dogs, he lost his ability to think rationally. Using his remaining 5% of power, he descended upon the pack of vicious hounds…

Chopping madly!

Instantly, great streams of blood covered the sky!

The streets were awash in blood!

Blood was everywhere.

The blood did not belong to Hiro, nor Ying Ming or Xiao Yu -- it was from the twenty dogs!

In an instant those giant dogs were ripped apart by Hiro's bare hands. Fragments of their dismembered bodies lay strewn everywhere. Some had their spines snapped, while others were disemboweled. It was horrifying to see!

All twenty dogs were instantly killed! The villagers were shocked that this normally nice and calm sixteen year-old boy had such power!

Even Ying Ming and Xiao Yu were stunned! Hiro had never killed anything, so they never knew he could be so merciless, all to save them…

"Big brother..."

Rich Man Gu was scared out of his wits, and his knees grew weak as his arrogant manner disappeared!

He saw Hiro glare at him with malicious intent and fire bursting from Hiro's eyes, Gu screamed, "Ah! Don't kill me! Ah! I beg you don't kill me!

"Your white robe... I'll give it back right now!" He grabbed the white robe from the hands of a maid behind him, and hurriedly tossed it back to Hiro. But Hiro did not accept it.

Rich Man Gu now feared for his life, "Ah! You don't want your clothes? Do you want money? Okay, I will give you how ever much you want! Just let me go!"

Hiro looked at him coldly, and said solemnly, "Don't insult me with your money! Money is meaningless to me! How many people have you killed with your riches and your beasts?"

Rich Man Gu was silent; he didn't know how to answer. But from his eyes, Hiro already found the answer!

Hiro continued coldly, "Just as I thought! You are worse than your dogs! Someone like you who cares only for money, and not for the lives of others, is worse than a swine! There is no reason for trash like you to continue living in this world. I will KILL you!"

Gu turned to run, but he was not as fast as Hiro! Hiro picked up a severed dog head from the ground and threw it -- mouth first -- towards Gu's head!

With a bone crunching sound, the dog's sharp teeth pierced through the back of Gu's head and shattered his skull. Rich Man Gu was instantly killed!

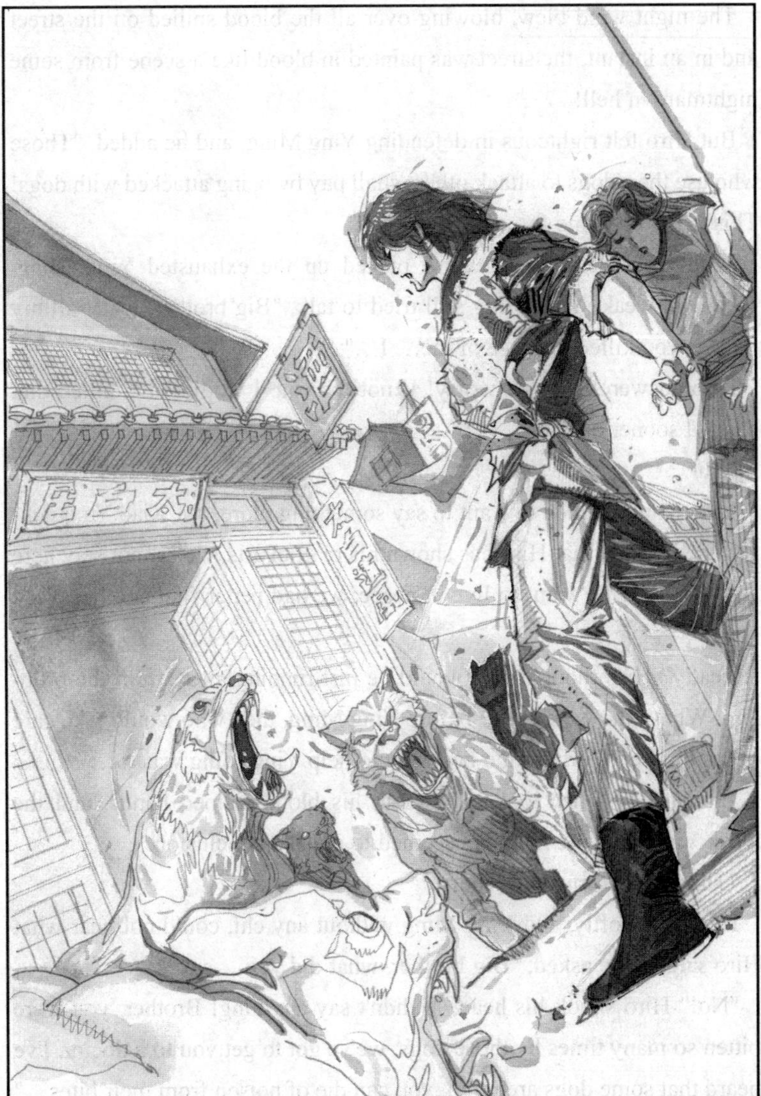
太白居

The night wind blew, blowing over all the blood spilled on the street and in an instant, the street was painted in blood like a scene from some nightmare in hell!

But Hiro felt righteous in defending Ying Ming, and he added, "Those who use their dogs to attack others shall pay by being attacked with dogs! This is the outcome for such a person."

With his speech ended, Hiro picked up the exhausted Ying Ming. Although weak, Ying Ming still tried to talk, "Big brother, it's… all my fault… you killed because of me… I…"

Hiro answered, "Don't worry! If not for you, I would have killed that bastard sooner or later!"

"But…"

Ying Ming seemed to want to say something more, but Xiao Yu quickly added, "Now that Hiro has shown his martial arts, we cannot stay here any longer. If we want to live in peace, we had better find another place soon!"

Really? Hiro thought that would be just running away from the problem. What if he were to die before Ying Ming, then who would take care of his brother? Perhaps the best way to help Ying Ming was to…

"Phoenix…" Hiro looked down at his blood stained hands, and the weak Ying Ming he held. He seemed to reach a conclusion.

"The phoenix must be reborn."

He said it softly, and Ying Ming without any chi, could not hear what Hiro said, so he asked, "Big brother, what did you… say?"

"No!" Hiro shook his head, "I didn't say anything! Brother, you were bitten so many times by those dogs, we've got to get you to a doctor. I've heard that some dogs are rabid, you can die of poison from their bites…"

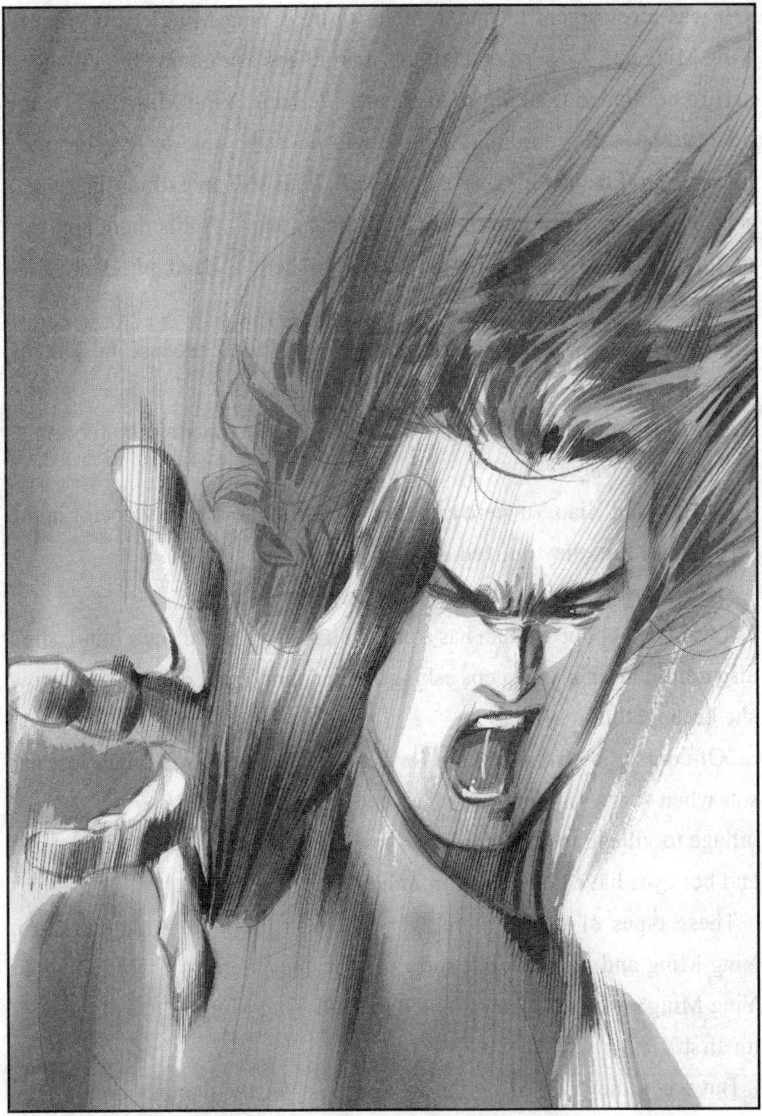

It was most urgent to find a doctor to treat Ying Ming! Hiro grabbed Ying Ming and Xiao Yu and left, his martial arts astounding the villagers!

Hiro continued thinking in his heart, "Perhaps, Ying Ming and I were both wrong... Extraordinary people will never be able to lead ordinary lives. Even if he lost his martial arts skill, he is still an extraordinary person. It is sad to force him to live an ordinary life... But is there any way in this world to restore his abilities? To help a dead phoenix... Be reborn?"

This question did not stay long on Hiro's mind, because he already found the answer!

Quickly, something made him decide to help the phoenix be reborn.

Something tragic...

As Hiro and Xiao Yu were carrying Ying Ming to the only doctor in the village, Dr. Lin, they noticed a crowd surrounded his house.

"How terrible!" the gathered villagers whispered.

"Yeah! That poor woman has a broken leg, and I heard she's blind, she's also a little insane, she keeps asking for her son! Yeah, do you know how she became this way?"

"Of course, it's from looking for her son! I heard that woman lost her son when she was young, so she went crazy, and she's been going from village to village looking for him. Now one of her legs has become lame and her eyes have gone blind from her tears of sorrow..."

These types of stories were everywhere in the land. Although Hiro, Ying Ming and Xiao Yu felt sorry for her, they were still worried about Ying Ming's wounds. They wanted to send Ying Ming in to see the doctor first.

But when they passed by the villager to enter the doctor's home, they heard the villagers say, "Speaking of which, we don't even know that poor woman's name. What's her son's name again? We can watch out for her!" The villagers were all kind-hearted. They wanted to help!

"Well, her name is Autumn *something*, I don't remember! But she was looking for her son, and his name is really special; he is called Wei, or Hero!"

Hero Wei? Hero Wei? Wei… Hero?

These words struck like lightening! Like Lightening! Hiro, Ying Ming and Xiao Yu were stunned! Blood froze in their veins! Ying Ming began to sweat and felt the blood of his kinship rise. Of all the places in the world, he finally heard news of… *her*? The person who is forever on his mind, who he has always wanted to meet… *her*!

Xiao Yu in shock, asked, "Wei… Hero? Brother Ying Ming, isn't that the name… your birth mother picked for you? So the poor woman they are talking about is your…?"

Xiao Yu did not need to speak further; Ying Ming already knew this must be the mother he has been separated from for sixteen years!

Hiro knew what Ying Ming was thinking, and he immediately turned and asked the villagers, "Excuse me, Madame, the woman you are speaking of, where is she now?"

The villagers spoke, "Oh her? She's such a poor woman! She said she's been looking for her son across thousands of miles. A couple of days ago she was here in our village. She was already limping and half-blind at the time. She contracted some kind of disease. She finally fainted here. But luckily it was in front of Dr. Lin's office, so he saved her. After checking her pulse, Dr. Lin found out that she had been gravely ill for more than a month. She's already reached a critical stage of her illness; there was nothing more anyone could do for her. Dr. Lin took pity on her and brewed her medicine himself. But she snuck away while Dr. Lin was treating some patients in the afternoon. She must have gone off to look for her lost son again. She's already so ill, Dr. Lin is afraid that she might die at any time. He was so worried about her leaving like this, he's asked all of us here to help him look for her. You know, they've been gone for almost half a day now, it must be bad news…"

"Ah! The gods are always so cruel! That woman clearly loved her son very much, why did she have to lose him? Her illness is also fatal; I hope that before she dies, she is able to find her son -- even if it is only to see him one last time."

The villagers sighed and shook their heads.

Hiro, Ying Ming and Xiao Yu listened with sinking hearts…

Ying Ming finally had a chance to see his birth mother, but she had gone. They could never be together it seemed, always apart.

Hiro grabbed the still weak Ying Ming and told him, "Let's go!"

"Go?" Xiao Yu asked.

"Yes." Hiro answered, and looking towards Ying Ming he said, "If we stay here and wait for Dr. Lin to return, do you think they will find her? We should go look ourselves!"

With that, Hiro grabbed Ying Ming and Xiao Yu and began following a set of footprints that might have belonged to Dr. Lin!

The villagers saw Hiro carry in someone sickly, and they thought he might stop for some treatment, but then they left again. Only Ying Ming and Hiro knew how kind Hiro really was.

He was a true man! A man above other men! He would never give up hope!

He knew that although Ying Ming was still hurt, they should temporarily set that aside to look for Ying Ming's long lost mother! A wound of the body was never as terrible as a wound of the heart.

"Big brother..." Although Ying Ming did not thank him outright, he was thanking Hiro in his heart, because he knew that he would never be able to repay all of Hiro's kindness.

Everything, everything is in the unspoken word; all thanks have already been shown...

But Dr. Lin and the villagers had been looking for her for so long without any success. Hiro, Ying Ming and Xiao Yu had just started, so would they have any luck?

It was getting dark, and Hiro had to hold up Ying Ming. The three of them walked very slowly and the road was getting more overrun and desolate. There were no signs of Autumn.

But some things in this world cannot be explained. Even if Dr. Lin and the rest were not able to find her, it didn't mean Ying Ming and his group would not. Because Ying Ming was Autumn's son, there is always some unexplainable tie between mother and son...

Just as they were aimlessly searching, Ying Ming's chest suddenly felt a flash of heat, and his blood began to boil, when a very strange emotion assailed him...

There!

It's really there!

It is a feeling of kinship! Of close kinship!

He called out, "Big Brother."

Hiro glanced at him and asked, "Brother, you look strange, what's the matter?"

Ying Ming said, "It's… her!"

"Her?" Xiao Yu said. "Brother Ying Ming, do you mean your mother?"

"Yes." Ying Ming nodded, looking at a darkened forest far ahead. Slowly he said, "I… suddenly have this feeling. I feel that my… mother is there… in the forest ahead!"

"In that forest!"

Autumn is in that forest?

Hiro believed in Ying Ming's premonition, and he said, "All right! If you believe your birth mother is there in that forest, then we will tear that forest apart if we have to so the two of you can finally reunite!"

Hiro clutched Ying Ming tighter, and grabbed Xiao Yu with his other hand. He stomped on the ground and flew towards the forest!

The forest was extremely large and they felt like ants among the great trees. They were also afraid to lose Autumn's trail. Hiro used all his strength and flew with the two of them. He wanted to search through the whole forest. Tonight he would find her and help the mother and son reunite!

He believed that with his dedication, the heavens would not dare to split this mother-son pair apart!

He didn't believe in destiny!

But no matter how much he didn't believe, or how much he tried, it was a difficult task to find one lone woman in such a vast forest!

Hiro had been holding Ying Ming and Xiao Yu while running for almost an hour now, but she was no where to be found. His body and face shimmered with sweat!

No matter how much he wanted Ying Ming to reunite with his mother, he was still a mere mortal! Even a powerful martial artist would become tired after running for an hour while holding two people. Hiro only had 5% of his power, how much more tiring was it for him?

Ying Ming could not bear to see Hiro struggling to run while carrying both of them; but he knew that Hiro would never stop even if he asked!

But luckily, just when Ying Ming was worried that Hiro would collapse, there in the distance came a faint flicker of light!

Someone was lighting a fire there?

The three of them had been traveling in the dark forest for some time now. The light attracted them like a beacon of hope. Xiao Yu was overjoyed.

"There's light! Brother Hiro, Brother Ying Ming, maybe… Ying Ming's birth mother is there making a fire?"

There was no need to ask. Before Xiao Yu could finish her sentence, Hiro already rushed towards the curious fire. Using the last of his strength reserve, he rushed deep into the forest.

It was already burning low; it had been some time since the fire was lit.

The second thing they saw was an unkempt person kneeling by the fire!

This person sat unmoving, as if no breath stirred. Hiro, Ying Ming and Xiao Yu began to worry. The three of them all thought, if this was Autumn, then why isn't she moving? Is she already… Dead?

Their hearts sank, especially Ying Ming's heart. Because he already knew whom that person lying prone was. The person lying prone gave him such a deep feeling of kinship… It's her!

It has to be her!

Hiro glanced at Ying Ming and knew that he wanted to look at the figure on the ground, so he slowly approached. Xiao Yu followed, and everyone was anxious.

This was the birth mother that Ying Ming had wanted to meet all his life, the woman who gave all her hopes to him. Finally, the mother and son will reunite!

Hiro carried Ying Ming to the prone figure's side. Ying Ming had no strength left, so Hiro turned the figure over.

They could finally see her kind face, and see if she was as the villagers said -- gravely ill?

But when they saw the face, they stood in shock!

Xiao Yu said, "What...? Brother Ying Ming! How could this be?"

Not only Xiao Yu, but the normally calm Hiro also turned and asked Ying Ming, "What! Brother... How could this be? This person... How can this be your... Mother?"

What? So the person was not Ying Ming's mother Autumn?

Then why did Ying Ming feel a special sense of kinship with this person?

Ying Ming stared at the upturned face; he was shocked because the face was not that of a woman! It was the face of a... man!

The man looked to be around forty years of age; he was an unkempt male beggar! He smelled of alcohol. So this beggar merely fell asleep by his own fire!

But this was not Autumn, so why did Ying Ming feel something special towards him? The feeling of kinship grew closer and closer, as they all approached this person. But who was this beggar?

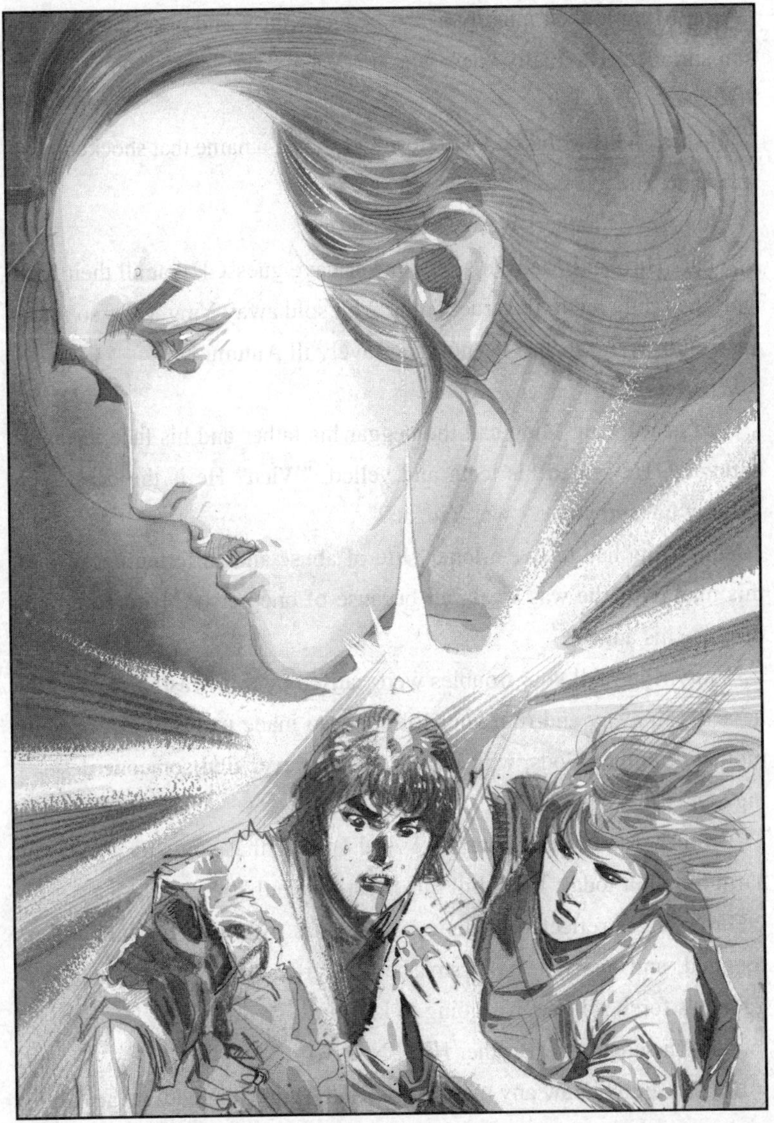

Ying Ming looked intently at the beggar's face, and a terrible realization surfaced! He finally knew who this was!

He's...

"He's..." Ying Ming said with fear and shock, a name that shocked Hiro and Xiao Yu.

"He is my... Father! Wei! Yaozhu!"

What? Hiro and Xiao Yu would never have guessed, that all their hard work had only led to the cruel father who sold away Ying Ming so many years ago. Wei Yaozhu! It's not the gravely ill Autumn!

Where is she?

Hiro heard Ying Ming call the beggar his father and his face instantly darkened. He gritted his teeth and yelled, "What? He is the beast of a father who sold you...? Wei Yaozhu?"

Ying Ming had to live a lonely life of abuse and suffering because of this man. Now he was weak, all because of one person. Hiro could not disguise his anger.

"Ying Ming! All your troubles were caused by this beast! Not only did he sell you away and ruin your life, he also made us lose track of your mother Autumn! Gods, why is that we can never find someone deserving? Only this beast?"

"Brother, I know you hate him! And I know that you still would not harm him, but today, I will kill this beast for you! "

Hiro's anger reflected in his eyes. He was merciless. A loud *woosh* sounded, and his right palm smashed towards Ying Ming's father Wei Yaozhu's forehead! He was going to kill him!

Xiao Yu screamed, "Brother Hiro! No! No..."

But she didn't know any martial arts, and Ying Ming had lost his ability. Who can stop Hiro from killing this man?

The palm strike rushed through the air blasting the hair from Wei Yaozhu's face. He was still too drunk to know!

But even if he were not drunk, he would not be able to escape!

He was certainly going to die now!

End of Volume 2

# STORM RIDERS

### by Wing Shing Ma

Storm Riders takes us on a journey through an amazing world in ancient China where, aside from the hegemony of the Royal Government, an individual and separate society exists: The World Fighting Association. Conquer, a powerful Kung Fu master, aspires to gain control of the Association and assembles the mightiest force of fighters known to humanity. Forgetting the evil deeds he's committed in his lifetime; he takes on Wind and Cloud, two very talented young martial artists, as his disciples. His destiny to be the Ultimate Master draws nigh; however, destiny has a will of her own and at the crux of the impending maelstrom blow Wind and Cloud...